T0270634

# THE
# COUNTERFEIT
# CHRISTIAN
### BEING AWARE OF THE ENEMY AND KNOWING YOUR TRUE PURPOSE

# LUIS LOPEZ

Order this book online at www.trafford.com
or email orders@trafford.com

Most Trafford titles are also available at major online book retailers.

Printed in Victoria, BC, Canada.

ISBN: 978-1-4269-3031-7 (sc)

ISBN: 978-1-4269-3640-1 (hc)

Library of Congress Control Number:  2010905813

*Our mission is to efficiently provide the world's finest, most comprehensive book publishing
service, enabling every author to experience success. To find out how to publish your book, your
way, and have it available worldwide, visit us online at www.trafford.com*

*Trafford rev. 4/26/2010*

 www.trafford.com

North America & international
toll-free: 1 888 232 4444 (USA & Canada)
phone: 250 383 6864 ✦ fax: 812 355 4082

# Contents

# FOREWORD

I am very pleased to be able to write this foreword for this wonderful book. Apostle Lopez is one of the finest men of God I have had the pleasure of knowing and love. The Apostle's insight into the Word of God and his prophetic gifts can only have come from God Himself. Together with his lovely wife and children they set the example for today's Christians and what we should strive for in our own walk with Christ. I'm sure you will grow to the next spiritual level simply by reading this wonderful book written by a wonderful man of God. I love you my brother in Christ.

1 Corinthians 15:58

**—DR. KEITH NESBITT SR.**
**FAITH BIBLE THEOLOGICAL SEMINARY**

# DEDICATION

To my **Lord and Savior Jesus Christ**, you have made me realize after all these years what real true love is. Thank you so much Lord God for being who you are, I love you so much. You have helped me to know who I am and how to really love my wife, others, and myself. I am so thankful. When the world engulfed me with its thirst, you are the Living Water that has always given me true drink. I sincerely thank you with all of who I am, and for the anointing to write this book for your people. You overwhelm me the closer I get to you, thank you so much Lord. You are so real!

To my wife, **Prophetess Michelle Lopez**, who has been there from the beginning, dealing with the intense and elongated hours I have poured into this book. You are the love of my life, and a powerful woman of God. You really are my best friend; I am so glad we met 20 years ago. My soul has a reason to live when I am with you. You have been there with me through the tough, hard, good, and crazy times. Thank you so much for believing in me with this project, and for helping me put it together. Your heart will always be part of mine always and forever. Loving you always to the very end of time.

To my Mother, **Naomi Hernandez-Lopez**, I would not even be here if it weren't for you. You are everything to me; there are no words to describe how much I really, truly love you mom. I will never forget the love, and the struggles you endured to deal with me and believe in me. Thank you for your prayers. Thank you for the wisdom and guidance you poured into me when I needed you the most; I love you.

To the rest of my family, I thank God for each and every single one of you. Love you all forever: **Josiah**, **Joel**, **Jose**, **Annamarie**, **Chelsea**, and **Dante**.

To **Dr. Keith Nesbitt, Sr.** Thank you for the opportunity and the information you have poured into me throughout the years. My family and I appreciate all the good you have shown us; I assure you it has not been in vain. Truly, without you this book would not have been possible. A million thanks. I love you brother.

# INTRODUCTION

The reason for writing this book is to prepare the Body of Christ for the coming Messiah. You must know who you are in Christ, and what you are capable of doing for the Lord while you're here on earth. In order for you to achieve the blessings of God and be victorious, you must follow the path plan of obedience and humility. In my writings you will read a lot about the heart, mind, and spirit to help keep you in alignment with the Word of God, positioning yourself to receive the blessings that have been waiting on you.

What you are about to read is going to equip, encourage, and prepare you, to become aware of the enemy's strategies and devious counterfeits which many times come in the form of people that you may have encountered in your everyday living. You will know the true meaning of your life in Christ when you keep away from such a crowd. For to long the devil has uprooted and torn down many born again believers into thinking they are worthless and cannot obtain their true function in life. You were created for more than just going through the motions and hoping one-day things will turn out for your good. Well your day is NOW!

The enemies' target and agenda is to bring confusion, striking the weak and faint hearted with all he has, causing the believer to lose route, impeding him or her from becoming the very thing God has called them to be. In the same sagacity, assisting the believer from a spirit of unwillingness and equipping the Christian that have faltered and forgotten who they really are with the proper tools to reach their purpose. The Adversary has sited himself to target and then assault those who are already in bondage. Therefore, carrying a canopy of blindness with him, placing it over the eyes of the Christian, to elude them from promises and unlimited blessings God has in store for your life.

Jesus Christ has commissioned me to be His "Apostle to the nations," mandating my wife and I, with the purpose and plan to bring true righteousness and holiness to the body of believers to this nation and around the world, preparing them for Christ's eminent return. In the same parallel, what John the Baptist had done for Christ in the First Coming—he prepared the way for the Lord—I shall do the same as he did, but for the Second Coming, by His command; I must be obedient. And in my obedience, I pray that this book and the anointing of the Holy Ghost fall on you as you read, and when you are finished reading, may the presence of God over flood you with His everlasting love, peace, and grace.

—LUIS LOPEZ
Rochester, NY

# GUARD YOUR HEART
# AND SPIRIT

# Chapter One

═══════════════════════════

# GUARD YOUR
## HEART AND SPIRIT

*Keep [Guard] thy heart with all diligence;*
*for out of it are the issues of life.*

**—Proverbs 4:23**

COMPARING THE REAL TO THE COUNTERFEIT tells you a lot about the imitation. The purpose is to fool the person into thinking that he has the same equal value as the original. But when you put both the counterfeit and the artificial into the Light, and if the replica does not have the eternal seal, the strip to prove its authenticity of being legitimately real, He will cast them into the Lake of Fire never to be received, heard, or seen again.

There are many believers who do not realize the infinite power that lies within the deepest part of who they really are. I pray that as you continue to read, your faith will be empowered, becoming sharper and more attentive of the enemy's devices and come to know your definitive purpose in this life. Whether it's through people, the supernatural, or both. We must continue to believe God. Many have swayed from the Lord and felt like life with Christ was not something to be part of. Christians, who once was on fire for God had given up or worse, have committed suicide. Countless others in the faith, and in the world have been deceived from the truth of God's Word for the so-called "good things" of this world, its system, and beliefs. Given into false hopes, visions, and dreams that promise new life, lots of money, or certain freedoms. In the end, all it has done was kill and destroy people's lives, some slowly and others quickly. The message I bring to you is reassurance, that the plan Christ has for you is greater than you can ever ask or think. Also to be aware of others who claim to be "saved and sanctified." They claim to be filled with the Holy Spirit, and some are filled truly, but engaged with a spirit that is not holy. As a matter of fact, it's a heart and spirit issue most of the time. We concentrate on the mind, but its also matters of the heart, the spirit, and the devil that need to be dealt with, or it could get us into unfathomable trouble. As we all know there are many thoughts running around in the minds of the believer. We must be scrupulous in how we confess those things into the ambiance of our environment, especially with other individuals inside and outside of our comfort zone.

## DID YOU KNOW

In college, I learned that the 'Heart' communicates with the brain through an inherent nervous system, assisting in making decisions, and influencing perception. It has a 40,000-neuron brain inside, which can learn, sense, feel and hold memory all by itself. Reminds me what Jesus said, "Out of the abundance of the <u>heart</u>, the mouth speaks," "For as he <u>thinks</u> in his <u>heart</u>, so is he," "For where your treasure is there will your <u>heart</u> be also."

What we don't hear from the ear of our heart too often is the fact that there are two plans available to mankind. God has a plan for your life, and the devil also has a plan for your life. One is for your destruction, and the other is for your good and life eternal. The lie of the devil is to steal your dreams, kill your relationships regardless if its marriage, corrupt friendships, sour businesses, or plainly preparing to get married. It is true what the Sacred Text commented about *our common* enemy who goes to and fro throughout the earth, to make sure no good comes to you (See Job 1:7; 1 Peter 5:8). This is the reason we must always be prepared spiritually and in the natural making sure when we start our hand-to-hand combat, which is prayer, we can go to war with assurance, boldness, holiness, and in the power of the Holy Ghost. If there is no prayer life with God, the enemy will mock you and you will become an easy target. Remember beloved, without a prayer life, your walk with Christ will be very short and will slowly fade and diminish. You have to do this every single day for the rest of your life. You cannot give up because Satan is not giving up on you, until you are gone from this life. He wants to make sure that God is nowhere to be found in your everyday thoughts. Meditate on these passages:

*The thief cometh not, but that he may steal, and kill, and destroy...*
**John 10:10** *(KJV)*

*For we wrestle not against flesh and blood, but against principalities, against powers, against the rulers of the darkness of this world, against spiritual wickedness in high places.*
**Eph. 6:12** *(KJV)*

*For the weapons of our warfare are not carnal, but mighty through God to the pulling down of strong holds; Casting down imaginations, and every high thing that exalteth itself against the knowledge of God, and bringing into*

*captivity every thought to the obedience of Christ; and having in a readiness to revenge all disobedience, when your obedience is fulfilled.*
**2 Cor. 10:4-6** *(KJV)*

*But if our gospel be hid, it is hid to them that are lost: In whom the god of this world hath blinded the minds of them, which believe not, lest the light of the glorious gospel of Christ, who is the image of God, should shine unto them.*
**2 Cor. 4:3-4** *(KJV)*

HERE ARE SEVERAL SCRIPTURES YOU CAN PRAY, TO SPEAK AGAINST THE ENEMY AND HELP YOU GUARD YOUR HEART, MIND AND SPIRIT:

*No weapon that is formed against thee shall prosper; and every tongue that shall rise against thee in judgment thou shalt condemn. This is the heritage of the servants of the LORD, and their righteousness is of me, saith the LORD.*
**Isaiah 54:17** *(KJV)*

*Have you an arm like God? Or can you thunder with a voice like His?*
**Job 40:9** *(NKJV)*

*He has shown strength with His arm; He has scattered the proud in the imagination of their hearts.*
**Luke 1:51** *(NKJV)*

*…For the battle is not yours, but God's.*
**2 Chron. 20:15** *(NKJV)*

*Your right hand, O LORD, has become glorious in power; Your right hand, O LORD, has dashed the enemy in pieces.*
**Exodus 15:6** *(NKJV)*

*Finally, my brethren, be strong in the Lord and in the power of His might.*
**Eph. 6:10** *(NKJV)*

*The eternal God is your refuge, and underneath are the everlasting arms; He will thrust out the enemy from before you, and will say, 'Destroy!'*
**Deut. 33:27** *(NKJV)*

*…Not by might nor by power, but by My Spirit, says the* LORD *of hosts.*
**Zech. 4:6** *(NKJV)*

## DISCERN THE COUNTERFEITS

The Counterfeit Christian comes in all different forms. *"Counterfeit"* meaning: to imitate, to forge, to feign, and to simulate. In these last days numerous people will admit to you that they are on the side of God. These people may well be relatives, believers from other religions, friends, or associates you highly respect. Apostle Paul, in 1 Corinthians chapter 12, wrote about the nine gifts of the Holy Spirit, which will help us make a distinction with these specific spirits, in people. This particular gift I'm going to mention is very important, just as the others. This gift is called "discernment of spirits." The *"Charismata"* in Greek is translated to: "Power, authority gifts." The Lord by His Spirit will establish these 'power gifts' to His children as He wills. It's very important to have this discernment, especially when you have individuals from all areas of life come into your circle. You cannot <u>always</u> have people touch, pray, and give you a word. We shouldn't always invite all different kinds of people into our homes either. Not every voice that says, "I love Jesus" is right in the eyes of our God. The Scriptures state "let no man put his hands on you suddenly" (1 Tim. 5:22). It is not to say that you should make everyone you encounter feel uncomfortable and offended. But, I am saying to be discerning and aware of your surroundings and who is surrounding you. Like a *Watchman*, a watchman is a *Seer*, or a prophet according to the Holy Writ. If you don't walk in the Spirit, with discernment, you would be inviting all different kinds of spirits into your home.

Remember that demonic spirits are spiritual hitchhikers. They cling to the ignorant and they follow, sleep, and hunt the weaker ones in the *Faith* (Hosea. 4:6). If you think, or feel you do not have this gift, or you have it, but you do not know how to execute the gift, pray and also speak to your leaders of your church for guidance to help you in that area. In the meantime, you can watch and see if their fruit is ripe and fresh to partake of it. When you do not take this seriously, the outcome can be devastating; mostly, people without their knowledge will start transferring spirits one to another. This is dangerous to the believer and the church. Please be very careful as the days begin to engulf us with its evil.

## GUARD YOUR SPIRIT

When you deal with believers, sinners, or making home and hospital visits, pray and anoint yourself with oil, if you do not know the people you are visiting or dealing with. Protect your spirit with the Word of God, to make sure your spirit and mind does not wander into places it shouldn't. Guard your gates, (ears, eyes, nose etc.) because it is not always easy to see when spirits try to attack you or attach themselves to you. *(That is why I spoke about discerning spirits)*. Why guard your gates? Because unclean spirits enter through your nose and mouth and when they are cast out, they come out of the same entrance as before. Proverbs 4:7 declares, *"Wisdom is the principal thing, therefore get wisdom, and in all your getting, get understanding."* I mention this passage given that we need the Wisdom and understanding of God and not man, in order to understand the realm of the Spirit. This is besides the everyday natural things. I am talking about things above and beyond human understanding and intellect. For example, like certain diseases that have no cure and doctors are in wonder themselves, and cannot explain why. Some physical ailments are actually spiritual, but it boggles the human mind and is therefore categorized by doctors as unexplainable. Therefore, causing humans to fall along the lines of ignorance, becoming unaware that demons and devils travel and follow people around in the spirit, and harass them. Factually, sometimes on a day to day and night after night basis, having no clue what is really going on with them, their household, or their children.

I would hear statements like: "I don't know what it is about them or this house, but I feel uncomfortable." Or, "I feel like something bad is going to happen if I stay and don't leave." Sometimes you become frustrated, feel angry, get headaches, feel sick all of a sudden, or spit up blood. This is a spirit of witchcraft, anger, a strong fence of warlock, rebellion, and stubbornness, coming against you. Others simply lack prayer. You know you need to pray, when you feel the unction of the spirit, but its like you are being squeezed, and it affects your prayer life. The slave girl, or "damsel" in the Book of Acts, was named "Alpithia." She had a spirit of divination called "Python," or "Apollo" which in Greek is *"Pythian Apollo,"* when translated from Greek to English (Acts 16:16). This spirit of python slithers its way into the Christian and the unbeliever's head, wrapping itself with the objective of constricting and choking the Word of God and prayer out from their hearts and minds, causing them to be unfruitful and lacking. (Come against it and fight back and keep the Word with all that is within you, because The End is near).

*Now he who received seed among the thorns is he, who hears the word, and the cares of this world and the deceitfulness of riches choke the word, and he becomes unfruitful.*
**Matt. 13:22** *(NKJV)*

*Now the ones that fell among thorns are those who, when they have heard, go out and are choked with cares, riches, and pleasures of life, and bring no fruit to maturity.*
**Luke 8:14** *(NKJV)*

In the days we live in, this is *one* of countless spirits that causes you to struggle to read God's Word and pray. And when you are about to open up your Bible and read, you don't know what to read, with all sorts of interruptions coming in every direction. The baby, the kids, the phone rings, this is going on, that is falling apart, you name it, disruption surrounds us all. This proves to the reader, there is a spiritual war that is beyond all of our imagination combined happening in the supernatural. Unfortunately, there are a lot of believers who do not believe in the spiritual realm, denying that hell or the devil even exists. Of course, God is more powerful than anything He created or in existence, but we do not want to be ignorant to the fact that evil spirits exist.

## CLEAN HOUSE

Demonic spirits occupy the six spheres and the second heaven. If you are one of the many others who need guidance in order to realize what is necessary and help you in your walk with Christ, below are some reasons concerning why these attacks occur:

- Living in disobedience or partial obedience

- No awareness/ignorance

- Necromancy, a practicing medium, sorcery

- White and black magic (witch, warlock)

- Demonic video games, movies, certain TV shows, etc.

- False religion, idol figures or figurines

- Santeria, witchcraft, wicca/wiccan, or voodoo

- Books, statues, demonic pictures/images, Ouija boards

- Generational curses/pride/spirit of leviathan

- Familiar spirits *(Acts 4:7, Isa. 19:3)*

- Desert spirits/Animal spirits/Animal sacrifices *(Isa. 34:11-15)*

- Don't believe Satan/Devil exists

- Rejection of Jesus Christ as Lord and Savior

- Spiritual birds/fowl *(Eccl. 9:12)*

## CURSED OR NOT CURSED, THAT IS THE QUESTION?

We are spirits having a human experience. Many believers and the world convey these spirits are just in our head, and explain it away into unbelief. Now that you are aware of these things according to the list, you should pray and seek out guidance. Someone in your church like a pastor or minister should set a date to visit your residence and begin the process of closing open portals, cast out all evil and unclean spirits, and anoint your home. I knew some friends who were believers, messing around with an Ouija board to see if it's real. Christians, no less! They thought it was just fantasy, a game of make believe, but as time went by they realized that it did work. Things don't just fall off from the center of the table, touch your body, speak to you audibly, or float in the air all by themselves! In addition, more demonic stir would invade and devilish entities speaking to them would transpire in their home, as terrible visions and a few other overwhelming evil activities, would torment them. Ultimately, I discontinued from visiting their home and had a pull to educate myself to be aware of these unclean practices. I did feel bad for them, being a young Christian I had no idea what to say or handle such things. They wanted to be free from it, and I really didn't have a clue how to deal with supernatural issues like that one. One thing I've learned studying about cults and the occult, you **NEVER** burn, or discard, an Ouija board where it can be seen; you throw it in a river, or a deep pit where no one would find it. If you burn it you will curse yourself, and you shouldn't give it away to someone else. Those spirits will fall on the person who finds it. These spirits are dangerous and life threatening. Evil spirits do not dally with you at all they play for keeps, and the prime objective is to have your soul in hell forever. In all seriousness, God does not have time to play, time is running out! Christians, who claim to know Him, really know of Him, and do nothing He says. Certainly, millions of people have no idea what we are up against. The invisible realm is more powerful than we are in comparison with the natural. Scientists say, in the 6th dimension we can eat an orange from the inside out. Imagine that!

## REVELATION: THE ENEMY'S PLAN

This reminds me of a revelation the Lord showed me a few years ago that brought me to my knees. The Holy Spirit took me to the 11th dimension of the spirit realm, and I saw Jesus Christ sitting on His throne in heaven. The Mighty God (Isaiah 9:6) just sitting there above the heavens and the earth was breathtaking and Glorious! Writing about Christ sitting on His Throne in heaven, stirred my recollection of watching a program about NASA, its scientists, and theory on physics. According to astronomers and astrophysicists they claim they have reached the end of the universe to the farthest northern point. Now, if you were familiar with numbers, you would find that if you were to stack a trillion dollars in one hundred dollar bills on top of each other, it would stand about 739 miles above the earth. Having that in mind, NASA continued their phenomenal discovery that the end of the universe is one hundred and eighty-seven trillion billions of miles, imagine that in one hundred dollar bills. In conclusion, pertaining to my own personal research and with over 55,000 hours of reading, hearing, and studying God's Word, I believe the Lord's heaven is in the North, in the constellation "Swan," according to the Scriptures and astronomical studies (*astrology is the perversion of astronomy*). As I studied the Holy Text and seeking the Lord with much prayer, you can perceive it is evident what the enemy was conjuring up in his mind to come against the Lord. Satan and the fallen angels tried to take the Father's position with a military tactic to bring down The Creator, from His Throne in heaven. He tried to outsmart and skirt God by flanking Him "in the sides of the North." Satan's plan failed, of course, confirming what Jesus said in the gospels; He saw Satan fall like lightning to the earth.

*I saw Satan fall like lightning from heaven.*
**Luke 10:18** *(NKJV)*

This is the revelation I have received from the Word, but I understand not everyone will be in the same mind of belief. I recognize the fact that heaven is northward, but to say exactly where in the North, no one truly knows unless we are there.

*For thou hast said in thine heart, I will ascend into heaven, I will exalt my throne above the stars of God: I will sit also upon the mount of the congregation,* **in the sides of the north**.
**Isaiah 14:13** *(KJV)* Emphasis added.

## ALL JOKES ASIDE

Beloved, lets not take His Word for a joke. We need to get it together. Heed to what the Lord commands, stay away from the enemies devices. One of the enemy's schemes, which are considered one of the most powerful deceptions, is to lead people into thinking he doesn't exist. This is how he deceives you, causing you to think it's merely the person we are dealing with, when their is much more influencing that individual. A lot of religious people have a hard time following the Lord. My prayer for you is if you are struggling in your walk with the Lord contact a leader or your pastor immediately. Let him guide you or assign someone into your life to help you in your journey with Christ. Allow the pastor to choose someone in whom you could be held accountable to, so when you need help, it's accessible. Remember the words Jesus proclaimed; we must make sure we are doers of the Word and not hearers only, deceiving ourselves. We must follow His Word and do what He instructs us to do.

*But why do you call Me 'Lord, Lord,' and do not do the things which I say?*
**Luke 6:46** *(NKJV)*

*Hypocrites! Well did Isaiah prophesy about you, saying: 'These people draw near to Me with their mouth, and honor Me with their lips, but their heart is far from Me. And in vain they worship Me.*
**Matt. 15:7-9** *(NKJV)*

*Be sober; be vigilant; because your adversary the devil walks about like a roaring lion, seeking whom he may devour.*
**1 Peter 5:8** *(NKJV)*

## SPEAK DEATH!

The vicissitudes of religion and its founders will never disprove who the God of the Bible is. The God of Abraham, Isaac, and Jacob; the only one true God. Although, we recognize false doctrine, we must embrace the truth no matter the pessimistic outcome of unbelief. We have to remain in a place of holiness in order to be used by the Spirit of God, to implement righteousness to those walking in error and a different spirit. Virtually, these counterfeit delusions of Scripture are close to the countenance from the words of the Great Architect, because they take from the Holy Bible to build their case, and yet so far away. Causing them to become blind guides and heretics, not knowing they are blind and will not be able to see nor grasp the light of the surefire Gospel of Christ.

I hearten the believer to relentlessly stay true to the Creator of your youth, weathering the storms of diverse kinds of adversity and indifference. The world will mock you even if you are a businessman, professional, or churchgoer. The devil makes no adjustments for you. Whether people say, "Hosanna" or "Crucify," you keep striving diligently on the narrow path that leads to life eternal (See Gal. 6:9). Nevertheless, we who are chosen need to pray, read, fast, and consecrate ourselves to make sure that we are hearing the voice of heaven and obeying Him. It could be very obstinate at times, but we need to stop confessing that it's too hard and we can't do it. Perhaps, if we refuse to speak this way our walk might just become a little easier.

*I can do all things through Christ who strengthens me.*
**Phil. 4:13** *(NKJV)*


The devil hears you and hangs on to every word that comes out of your mouth; make sure you do not become superfluous with your words. He is our antagonist, an adversary who tries to bring destruction with all kinds of circumstances and situations to prevent you from going further. We often quote certain combat verses, such as, "speak life" to battle and resist negative and erroneous conditions in your verve as you live your life for God. Let me take it further, we need to also speak death! Speaking death to those things that should not be living in your life will start to improve your grounds of spiritual awareness, you will notice breakthroughs will begin to explode and embark a new fervor, setting you in motion in order to subsist with sweet victories. Speak death to that cancer! Speak death to all destructive relationships and soul ties in your life (See Prov. 18:21). In God's eyes it is very crucial for us to do His will. His plan is so much better than ours. Do His will at all costs no matter the expenditure involved. To God be all the Glory and Honor! I guess the real question is, are you willing to pay the price? Never give up on speaking life and death into your volatile situations and watch how the Lord will turn it around for your good.

*Death and life are in the power of the tongue, and those who love it will eat its fruit.*
**Prov. 18:21** *(NKJV)*

## IT'S NOT FAIR

Unfortunately, as a parent, we always want to be there for our children and protect them. There was a man, who was terrible to a lot of people on our street, and this man had a son who went to the same school from our neighborhood. Some of the boys in class knew that this is the man's son. Every time the boy walked home from school they would take their frustrations out on him and beat him up, just because of his father's bad attitude.

It's not fair that the son had to pay for his father's behavior, but its true we get judged for all kinds of things. It could be from our appearance, or the kinds of clothes we wear, cars we drive, or plainly identified with someone we love and speak too. This is the heart of Satan; he hates the fact that we look, talk, and sound like Jesus Christ. Satan, with all that he has in his arsenal tries to stop us from speaking God's Word, especially through tough times and tribulation periods. He is always on the prow to destroy us, trying to cause all kinds of hurt and harm our way with no remorse in his heart, and believe me he has no heart. Christians sometimes don't have even a hint how to handle his tactical approach and they give up on God because the fire was too hot to bear. The trials are many and continuous, but as you well know, one would end just for another to rise up in its place. I was brought up with the saying, "Tough times don't last, tough people do." Deplorably, on a vast scale, you will meet many who will become bitter and very angry for all the unexplainable troubles they had to endure. You must be careful how you exhibit your anger with others and particularly toward God. This might sound funny but sometimes we have to forgive God too.

It is iniquitous to live that kind of lifestyle and retaining an angry heart toward God and others. We are commanded by the Lord, to Love Him and our neighbors with all that we have in us. I have found approximately thirty-one "love one another" in the Scriptures. No matter what kind of a neighbor they are to you, or others, we must learn to love them as ourselves and this is not always easy to do. As time goes on and as you get closer to God, he gives you the grace to pursue and follow His commandment. It is difficult to live a life of total humility, always determined to saunter after the spirit and not get offended, or upset, or say things we shouldn't say or even do things that should not have been done.

When I had the privilege to meet a well-known author, speaker, and anointed man of God, Mike Murdock in Buffalo, New York several years ago, he told me one thing that I will never forget. First he gave my wife and I a word for our children, and then he spoke a word to me personally, it changed my whole way of thinking with my walk with Christ. It was such a simple word, but it meant the world to me at that time. Ever since he spoke that word to me, I always kept it in the back of my mind. I was going through a lot of different types of issues with my family then, and that one small word just stood out, and I would repeat it and kept it in my prayers ever since. I have learned that a Word from God in season will build you up, and a Word out of season will do more harm then good. We must be sensitive and obedient when He speaks through His anointed ministers and also learn to heed His still small voice in our prayer closet. This way we can learn when to speak the Word and when to retain it as we go forth.


## ARE WE ALL CHILDREN OF GOD?


The Scriptures states, the world does not know us because they didn't know Him (Jesus), and they really don't know who we are either; for the reason they are spiritually dead and their ears are stopped—this verse does stand till this day. According to the Bible, when speaking about God and His children its always referring to, a sign of intimacy and relationship, like a parent to a child. He would not separate them into two different categories in the chapters of the Bible. Plus, they would be walking in the admiration of reading His Word, spending time with Him, loving Him, ministering His Word to others. They do not have any desire to give their lives just yet to the Lord, even though they know in their heart of hearts they need to. Some are deceived and this is when prayer comes in.

A particular young man said to me one day after service, as we were conversing about religious matters, "Why should I go to church when it's full of hypocrites?" When he said that, I replied, "That is cool how you are able to discern something so negative like that, if you give your life to Christ you can demonstrate how not to become a hypocrite and lead them by example?" The person stayed quiet for a moment, thought about it, knowing he had at one time or another been a hypocrite himself. This is not to condemn anyone but to cause people to think. Winning an argument is easy sometimes, but it's not worth losing the relationship. Speaking the truth with love and gentleness in humility is the key. In actuality, we are informed to continuously attend church service; we are to assemble ourselves accordingly. (Hebrews 10:25)...*Not forsaking the assembling of ourselves together, as is the manner of some, but exhorting one another, and so much the more as you see the Day approaching.*

*But ye, brethren, are not in darkness, that that day should overtake you as a thief. Ye are all the children of light, and the children of the day: we are not of the night, nor of darkness.*
**1 Thess. 5:4-5** *(KJV)*

*Behold what manner of love the Father hath bestowed upon us, that we should be called children of God; and such we are. For this cause the world knoweth us not, because it knew him not. Beloved, now are we children of God, and it is not yet made manifest what we shall be. We know that, if he shall be manifested, we shall be like him; for we shall see him even as he is.*
**1 John 3:1-3** *(ASV)*

The verse above states that those who are not children and watch for Christ's return are in darkness of His coming and understanding. We who are saved are in the light and will watch for His coming.

We are described as a peculiar people, a Holy Nation, who looks forward to Christ's second Coming. The second coming is **invisible**; His third Coming will be **visible** at the end of the seven-year tribulation period. I know theologically, the *rapture* is not popularly known as the "second coming" however, so we can understand it as a whole, in total doctrine it is true, and the rapture which is invisible will not fall along the lines as dogma, for the reason it is true and proven according to the Word of God.

As I was saying earlier, getting back to my point, this is not a license to condemn, judge, or give up on people, God forbid! Regardless if they are children of God or not, whether they believe in the rapture, or whether its post tribulation or mid tribulation, we must intercede and speak those things that are not, as though they were (Rom. 4:17) and guide them who are not strong in the Lord to edify those who are not. We must have an understanding, especially toward our own loved ones with much passion, commitment, and constant prayer, no matter who they are or what they've become: family, friends, or even our enemies. It's all about **souls** and love, loving them into the knowledge and kingdom of our Lord Jesus Christ, His Spirit, for the "Rejoicing" of His Father.

*The fruit of the righteous is a tree of life, and **he who wins souls** is **wise**.*
**Prov. 11:30** *(NKJV)* Emphasis added.

*Let him know, that he, which converted the sinner from the error of his way,* ***shall save a soul from death***, *and shall hide a multitude of sins.*
**James 5:20** *(KJV)* Emphasis added.

Speaking of rejoicing, for over three decades I was taught that it was the angels who would rejoice over a sinner who repents and comes to God. When you read this carefully it distinctively says, *"There is joy In the presence of Angels"* this means, Jesus and the Father are throwing a party, and most likely Saints who have passed on. Praise God!

*Likewise, I say unto you, there is joy **in the presence of the angels of God*** *over one sinner that repenteth.*
**Luke 15:10** *(KJV)* Emphasis added.

I am so glad that the blood of Christ has cleansed us from sin, guilt, shame, and the stains of our past, handing down countless reasons why we must read and obey the Lord. He wants a real relationship with His children without having hatred, bitterness, and a sinful heart lurking in our members. He wants us to love and live a peaceful life. *"Blessed are the peace makers, and we will be called children of God."* (Matt. 5:9) He has a big plan for all His children, if we only heed to His voice. He is the only one who brings life, supporting us in all areas of our lives so we could function and become more like Him everyday.

The Lord said to me one day, "I resurrect death, I refresh what is stagnated, I am all that you need." That simply blew my mind. At that time, I needed to hear those exact words. He is always their taking care of His own. No one can say that I do not hear His voice or that you are not capable either. You belong to Him and He belongs to you. I say this with sincerity and consideration for you the reader. We understand God's children are those who are born again. Sons and daughters is a mature term, but we are His born again children as long as we stay obedient to Him and His will. Others outside of this understanding are His creation, and God does love them as well, but to earn the title as a "Child of God" and enter heaven you must be redeemed (See John 3:3). We must come from the darkness into the light, which is Christ. I know this is not popular coming from the pulpit or certain books, but this is biblical. I am sure you have tried everything by your own influence, and in the power of the Holy Ghost to be Holy and obedient to God. Nevertheless, you must remain open in a state of surrender from your will, for genuine liberation to visit and remain. You and I must always keep that in mind every day for the rest of our lives. Being a Christian is a lifestyle and relationship, not a religion.

Jesus Christ is still the same yesterday, today, and forever all at the same time (Heb.13: 8). This is true to its very essence, even God called Jesus, God, in the New Testament, claiming the status of His Son's position, validating who He was to give us strength to continue onward.

*But to the Son He says: "Your throne, O God, is forever and ever; a scepter of righteousness is the scepter of Your Kingdom. You have loved righteousness and hated lawlessness;* **Therefore God, Your God,** *has anointed You with the oil of gladness more than Your companions."*
**Heb. 1:8-9** *(NKJV)* Emphasis added.

In the same token, I know it's comforting and popular to call our love ones, children of God but all in all according to Scripture, they are not. Not everyone who professes Christ or called themselves Christians is in right standing with God. When we keep plugging into peoples minds that do not have Christ the hope of glory living in their hearts, the enemy tends to deceive them into thinking they are God's children. This is how the devil distorts their mind, so he could keep them from receiving Jesus as their personal Lord and Saviour. I have heard many preachers' kids who say, "Well Apostle Lopez, I am a child of God, and I go to church every Sunday faithfully, so I know I'm ok." In this scenario they claim that because their mother or father is a leader of a church or has a church, they have free access into God's heaven. In all cases this is never true, and its sad to say, in certain instances they are worse than sinners. The devil has a main target on his mind, and it's to subtract anything associated with you and the Lord's promises which are for you. As he lied to these P.K.'s I met, he is totally lying and deceiving them like never before and it is getting worse as the DAY approaches. It makes no difference to him who you are, or what church you belong to, he doesn't wait until you are filled with God's Word and the Holy Ghost and then attack you. He starts his all out assault when you are young and ignorant at a very early age. Notice, you never teach a child how to be bad and selfish, they already know how, we have to teach them how to be good and giving.

I have family that I hold dear in my heart, thinking the same way; because their parents go to church they are okay. It hurts me when I think about how they live, since I want nothing more but for all of my extended family to be saved. In reality, it's up to them to choose, and I pray that they will choose life soon, as it is mentioned in the Scriptures, and to choose now before its too late.

Since 1987, this has been an issue for a long time. When I ask, "Where will you go if you died right now?" Some have said, "To heaven," many replied, "to the ground and rot," and others said, "I'm not sure." These kind of basic questions give men and women something to think about after you witness to them. This is where evangelism steps in. Not everyone can evangelize and lead people into the kingdom. You have to be equipped and prepared for what's ahead of you. Jesus declared it's the 'gift and anointing' that He imparts for the believer to have the power to lead humans to salvation. We don't choose, He does the choosing and appoints us to go and bear fruit (See John 15:16).

## NO LIMITS

We are the only ones that do not have to work our way into heaven like the other false religions and false gods exemplify. I am not saying that we shouldn't work perceiving our faith without any works is dead, and works without faith is also dead. The Bible says anything that is not of faith is sin. My conclusion is we don't have to try so hard and kill ourselves trying to make it into heaven the price has been paid already. I thought to myself the other day and said, "How did Jesus pay a high price when He is God in flesh and when He died He was able to pick His life up again?" As soon as that thought entered into my head, the Holy Spirit said, "Son, I did pay a high price. I have given up my home and took the form of **man**, for the rest of eternity."

Basically, from what I understood, He ceased from transforming like He used to. I immediately understood what He was saying to me. Like in the Old Testament, He would become all these things, a burning bush, a pillar cloud by day and fire by night, a captain of the army of the Lord of Hosts with Joshua, and one of the three visitors entering into Abraham's tent, and others knowing Him and the Father are one in the same. Now, He is 100% Man, as well as 100% God. He told His disciples, "Its better for you if I leave, so the Father can send the Holy Spirit (comforter). It was all done so Jesus the Lord could be around the world at the same time, by bringing His Spirit to our planet. My understanding is to plainly know that Jesus can do whatever He wants, when He wants to do something that glorifies Him and His Father. Limiting God would sound foolish at this point in my life without the affect of recognizing that He is sovereign. My prayer to the Lord for you would be that God would help you succeed in all that you do according to His will, in addition to never put limits in what He can do, or has done. Unlimited is His name—GOD. I believe He prompted me so I do not allow any thought(s) to minimize who He is. I thank the Lord for that.

**TWO FATHER'S**

There are two fathers' that exist in our world today, the one in heaven and the one here on earth. Father God and the Father of lies (as we know one is real, the other counterfeit). We must bear the fruit of the Holy Spirit, to be able to differentiate who is who in these last days. Aren't you blessed that you and I decided to choose God over the devil? This is a blessing beyond human comprehension. It's a burden and a deep concern thinking about our loved ones making a decision to accept Christ as their Lord and Savior as we did. Do not allow yourselves to be deceived by the devil and his lies regarding you or that it is too late for your family to come to the Lord. Always pray for all of them and others to come to Christ, and you who are saved already to be equipped as you work out your salvation with fear and trembling.

*Work out your own salvation with* **fear and trembling**.
**Phil. 2:12** *(KJV)* Emphasis added.

*Serve the* LORD **with fear,** *and rejoice* **with trembling**.
**Psalms 2:11** *(NKJV)* Emphasis added.


## ATTIRE OF WAR

Make sure you put on the whole armor of God, if you do not, the enemy will have a soccer game in your mind. He doesn't play fair; he will make sure you will be open in your spirit for all different kinds of afflictions. As soon as you go to work it will not take very long before the devil shows his face. Here are some tips to help you confess and realize what this armor does for you. This is not in Scripture just for information, but the Spirit of God recorded this for a purpose to learn His ways of wisdom.

1. **Helmet of Salvation** - protects your mind from the fiery darts of the enemy. Plead the Blood of Jesus over your mind (soul), and pray for the Helmet of salvation to protect your Spirit. The soul and spirit are knit closely together. Remember your soul needs to be renewed; your spirit is already saved and becomes a new creation in Christ Jesus. Romans chapter 12 says that your soul–which is your mind–must be transformed, not your spirit. If you mix the two, it can lead to confusion, and God is not the author of disorder.

2. **Breastplate of Righteousness** - this piece of armor protects your heart. The Word constantly states, we

have a desperate and immoral heart, who can know it? God is always looking and examining our hearts. We must make sure that our heart is protected at all times. It's very important that we do not have unforgiveness or bitterness toward anyone. This is a HUGE hindrance in our walk with Christ. Guard your heart and most of all forgive everyone! (See Prov. 4:23)

3.  **Shield of Faith** - this will protect you when hell's agents come your way with a different Gospel message. Make sure you are walking in your faith. Your faith will please God and help you overcome the enemy's devices and become acquainted with your exact purpose. Without *stubborn faith* in Christ, you will leave the Lord and go back to your old ways. Jesus said, "If you leave your faith in God for another, even if it's your own, eight demons enter into you, and the last state of that man is worst than the first." (See Matt.12:43-45) Be a watchman, know that most times believing has a beginning and an ending, *Faith* always is. I will talk more about that later in the book.

4.  **Belt of Truth** - similar to the Shield of Faith. Jesus is the Truth. As long as He remains wrapped around your waist in the center of your body, you will always retain truth from within the depths of your spirit. Realize belts have different levels, so does the truth of His Word. Glory to glory, faith-to-faith, and strength-to-strength.

5.  **Sword of the Spirit** (The Word) - the spoken Word will always rebuke, expel, resist, banish, destroy, the works of the devil. Satan has no place to hide when you speak the eternal Word. The adversary hates it with a passion. A few Christians explained to me how demons would come and put their hands over their mouth as they are being attacked, so the name, JESUS won't come forth. Jesus **is** the Word, demons know the best way to assail

a believer is first covering his or her mouth. The Word cuts both ways like a two-edged sword, be prepared always and read your Word on a day-to-day basis.

6. **Gospel Shoes of Peace** - the steps of a good man are ordered by the Lord (Psalms 37:23). This piece of armor helps you know where you should and shouldn't go. So when the enemy comes against you and begins to bring chaos into your dwelling, you know how to step on him and bruise his head! He is always going to be under your feet forever! He has no future but you do.

## TRIALS AND TESTS

As you know already, tests will come and that is a promise from the Lord. So let your test be your Test-imony. There are 10,000 promises of God in the entire Bible, 3,000 in the Old Testament and 7,000 in the New Testament. The Scriptures are filled with promises to build you and I up. These promises are not all for our good. Some of these promises have consequences that pertain to breaking the law and bringing death to your doorstep. Now that I have become wiser, I ask God for His good promises. Allowing the flow of the eternal Texts of His promises to reverberate from my mouth, into the atmosphere of my home creating an environment of tranquility and hope. When you begin to act upon what He has already given you, you will see a variation in your attitude, particularly when trials come your way.

It's a sad thing when people start out good with the Lord, and then stop when the trials and tests of every day life come their way. When our faith is challenged it causes Christians to lose heart, refraining the believer from calling out to Jesus for help when they need to. We are nothing without Him. This is one thing the enemy used against me when I was a teenager.

I allowed the devil for years to come and make me feel like such a hypocrite in the faith, why continue? "You call yourself a Christian, and this is how you talk and act?" Get this; once you tell people you are a Christian, all eyes are on you. Like being attacked in the spirit wasn't enough, now here come hell's agents and counterfeit Christians ready to devour you in the natural. This was used to knock me down and discourage me like nothing ever could. As time went on, I became hungry and started to thirst for His righteousness once more. When Satan tried again, bombarding my thoughts with doubt and unbelief, I fought back with the written Word, just like Jesus did in the desert, knowing that Satan accuses and the devil slanders. Stop him at his word, for only Satan's words fall to the ground and will never stand against the Lord.

*The seed is the word of God. Those by the wayside are the ones who hear; then the devil comes and takes away the word out of their hearts, lest they should believe and be saved. But the ones on the rock are those who, when they hear, receive the word with joy; and these have no root, who believe for a while and in time of temptation fall away. Now the ones that fell among thorns are those who, when they have heard, go out and are choked with cares, riches, and pleasures of life, and bring no fruit to maturity. But the ones that fell on the good ground are those who, having heard the word with a noble and good heart, keep it and bear fruit with patience.*
**Luke 8:11-15** *(NKJV)*

## THE CALL OF GOD

The Lord reminded me and said, "Son, I knew you were going to sin in the future and I chose to save you anyway." "I have forgiven you for the sins you did in the past and present, and the sins you will commit in the future, they are all washed in my blood." (See 1 John 1:9). My face lit up like a Christmas tree, that statement brought so much freedom into my life!

I was a kid who was struggling, fighting to keep my faith. Holding on to Jesus as if my life depended on it, and literally my life did depend on it. Through everything I have gone through as I was hanging on, the Holy Ghost was the only one their for me. Sure, I had the pastor and his leaders in my church to guide and teach me, but for some odd reason its like I was invisible to certain people. The feeling was like the Lord was keeping me from being involved in assured conditions, being kept on the side for something greater in my life. Even though these weird feelings and thoughts were running in the back of my mind, I would ignore them and try to get involved in some type of helps ministry. So I asked the pastor if I could be involved in the food ministry. The following week one of the deacons came and allowed me to serve food for the homeless. Personally, I was happy the Lord used me to be a blessing to those in need. I made lots of friends while I was engaged in that ministry and I loved it. At the same time, having constant feelings I couldn't be around people on an everyday basis drove me crazy. The Lord would separate me from friends, Christians and family. I didn't understand certain events and difficulties I had to go through as a teenager, in particular when confusion of what God was doing to me came in and out of my mind. Later on, as I continued walking with Christ and the ministers He would divinely set in my path, the Lord began to give me the understanding of who I am.

Now I understand my Call and the trials that came my way, was all for my good. However, not everyone is called to be an apostle, prophet, or teacher. Not to say that no one went through something similar or worse than I. But when you are a teenager, full of energy, zealous, unlearned, want to hang out, eat everything in the fridge like a lion, you tend to want to be around friends, and have the great feeling that you are appreciated and important. It took time to understand the Call that God had for me. Now without a shadow of any doubt, I know now. Many didn't understand and others still don't, that's okay. It's not my job to convince anyone. There were times that I just felt like giving up, but I knew I had to hold on to the Call by hanging on with the strength He has given me.

*Now unto him that is able to keep you from falling, and to present you faultless before the presence of his glory with exceeding joy.*
**Jude vs. 24** *(KJV)*


## LIFE LESSONS

To tell you the truth, as the years went on it took everything inside me, every fiber of my being to hold on to Jesus. Trial after trial came my way constantly and didn't let up. Day after day, night after night, yelling out to Jesus to come and rescue me with tears streaming down my face. My father taught me a long time ago, with his philosophy saying, "Put your belt on tight son, men are not suppose to cry!" It took a long time to get that kind of thinking out of my head. For some reason, which I know it's the Lord, I really didn't believe that. I would whisper to myself and say, "I am not a robot without feelings dad, a real man cries, a real man shows emotions, and a real man serves God!" Not allowing that deadly spirit of pride control how I feel and think helped me in my walk with Christ. Further, if I didn't go through my brokenness period, I wouldn't have been married as long as I am now. Just ask my wife.

Trials, anguish, and tests came and caused me to be on my face before God, calling out His name and asking Him to help me. I kept hearing thoughts in my mind, "Your not saved, what you feel isn't real, its all in your head." I know you heard these thoughts at one time or another at work, school, church, or home. I am here to tell you the enemy is opening fire and disrupting your thought process with blazing darts into your mind, trying to get you off the narrow path. If you think about it, the **devil** cannot physically take you off this path of life. He is only trying to prevent you from damaging his kingdom so you can fall away from Christ, and utilizing every arsenal he has to make sure he prevails against you.

I believe you cannot lose your salvation, but you can give it up, and that is a slow fade. Imagine waking up one morning and you tell someone, "Oh my goodness, I just lost my salvation!" Personally, I don't agree with that statement on the basis that it is never once found in Scripture. Once more, the Word of God tells us to work out our salvation with trembling and with fear, simply because redundant behavior with sin will lead the person to backslide from God, but to just lose salvation; I cannot perceive that happening. Nevertheless, we must stay strong in the Lord and in the influence of His strength. Truthfully, we cannot go on acting like we are high and mighty, and holier than anyone else; we will lose potential souls instead of winning them for the Lord. We have to be very meticulous, cautious, and learn to choose our words wisely at all times. Proverbs tell us, "In the multitude of words, sin is not absent." This verse and most of these righteous and moral values in 'the proverbs' start in the home, learning to become examples one to another, with a clear conscience lifting our hands without wrath or doubting. Again, since we can't just lose our salvation, if you are continually sinning, you will lose at the end and die. The Bible says, after sin is complete it brings forth death. I am reminded of Samson when he kept playing around with sin, and Delilah, eventually it all ended up short for Samson. He became prideful thinking he had power of his own accord, until the Philistines who are now called Palestinians, came upon him. Clueless, to the idea the Lord would ever leave and abandon Samson, he was forsaken; the Philistines chained and severely punished him, including plucking his eyes out.

Anyone who revels with God and His anointed; you will end up in a place you cannot come back from.

*Do not touch My anointed ones, and do My prophets no harm.*
**Psalms 105:15** *(NKJV)*

When you read the Book of Judges, you will read Samson kept lying to Delilah, about where his strength lies, until he ended up telling her the truth. He did not know the Spirit of the Lord left him. In the meantime, he kept telling her all different kinds of stories where his strength came from. In one instance he said to Delilah, "If you tie me up with these kinds of ropes then I will lose my strength." In his insolence and superciliousness, claiming that his power came from his own authority, he lost it and became like any other man. Evidently, Samson was highly persuaded by evil desire, and lastly revealing to Delilah the secret about his hair. This was a very hard "life lesson" for Samson. (Judges 16:1-31).

Friends, do not play with "Delilah," staying far away from a spirit that will manipulate you like what you just read is the best thing you can ever do. It gives a great meaning for the old saying, "If you play with fire you will get burned, literally."

No matter the cost, always guard your heart and your spirit!

# CHAPTER TWO

# THE VALLEY OF BROKENNESS

# Chapter Two

====================

# THE VALLEY
## OF BROKENNESS

*The Lord is near to those who have a broken*
*heart, and saves such as have a contrite spirit.*

**—Psalms 34:18**

IT'S IN MY HEART TO WRITE about the "Valley of
Brokenness," knowing it's desperately needed in the Body of
Christ today. Multitudes of Saints have fallen off the path of
life. Whenever my wife and I would minister and mentor other
couples and singles God would place in our path, the subject
of brokenness and humility always came up. We began to
see their countenance fall and they became fearful when I
proceeded to elucidate the fact, brokenness is necessary in
the heart of **every** Christian believer. On numerous occasions
we can see a change in their spirit and a façade will start to
form over them and take their entire guise and character to
an unusual level of disappointment. I explained to them, that
God would be hindered, with the understanding; He does
not use prideful and arrogant people. When you are walking
in the cloud of pride, it will cause destruction to yourself,
and others around you. If I were to put an individual who
deals with either pride, secret sin, or has a spirit of always

lying–on the 21ˢᵗ floor of an office building, and another on the 2ⁿᵈ floor, they eventually would find each other. Ultimately, these prideful, sinful, and lying spirits will come into contact and connect one to another some way or another. Pride comes before a fall the Bible tells us. This is why we need the Holy Spirit to help change us, so when we do need to cry out to God and plead the blood of Jesus to be better in our circumstances and lives He would hear us, especially in our most hurting and desperate time of trouble.

Ironically, when change begins with its cousin *Mr. Uncomfortable*, we start to rebuke and destroy the works of the enemy. When it is really God who was doing it by honoring your prayer the night before, when you were asking Him to change you and your ways. I have come to the conclusion; the person really doesn't want to change for the better. Being comfortable is comfortable, and not wanting anything or anyone to remove them away from their comfort zone. My inquiry is how will God be able to do all these wonderful things for you and through you, if you don't want to pay the price? And, are you willing to forfeit the cost, and refuse to become broken? One reason why many get fearful is because the process of becoming broken really hurts. It's better for you to humble yourself than for God to do it. When God does it, Whew! It results in suffering. Humiliation is part of humility. Like I said before in the previous chapter. Love is humble. Love never fails, and it covers a multitude of sins. Prayer is very important in your life. God loves you more than words can ever show or demonstrate. It would take eternity for God to show you how much He loves you, which is why you have to live in a body that never dies or gets old. Since God is eternal and His love is eternal, it's going to take eternity to show you His charity. His capacity to love is greater than yours, and his capacity to hurt is greater than yours. You have to submit and be humble in the sight of your God. Take into consideration to allow yourself to ask for brokenness in prayer, instead of allowing the Lord to do it; it will go well with you.

*Humble yourselves therefore under the mighty hand of God, that he may exalt you in due time.*
**1 Peter 5:6** *(KJV)*

*Humble yourselves in the sight of the Lord, and He will lift you up.*
**James 4:10** *(NKJV)*

*For whosoever exalteth himself shall be abased; and he that humbleth himself shall be exalted.*
**Luke 14:11** *(KJV)*

*The eyes of the LORD are on the righteous; And His ears are open to their cry. The face of the LORD is against those who do evil, to cut off the remembrance of them from the earth. The righteous cry out, and the LORD hears, and delivers them out of all their troubles. The LORD is near to those who have a broken heart, and saves such as have a contrite spirit. Many are the afflictions of the righteous, but the LORD delivers him out of them all.*
**Psalms 34:15-19** *(NKJV)*

## CONSECRATE ME, MY LORD, AND MY GOD

You don't hear about consecration coming from the pulpit, its very rare that you do. The word *"Consecrate,"* is a term, meaning: to make pure, holy, consecrate, set apart, devoting oneself to God, to regard as sanctification. This is when you separate yourself from the noise, devoted to God completely, with your time. Looking to see what is the will of God for your life. No whining and complaining about how lonely you are, or how you need to be around people. This is between just you and the Spirit. Walking in total subjection to His will and plan. We must always come to God with a humble heart on a day-to-day basis. This is how we conquer the enemy. This is how we are able to meditate on His Word. This is how we become obedient and willing. If you do not humble yourself and become broken so He could pour out His anointing through you on an internal level, He will expose you and break you on an external level. That love process will be very painful and humiliating at times, but rewarding when it is over. Men and women, who are specifically and specially commissioned, will not have the luxury of fitting in with the world at great levels. There will be instances when people won't understand you since they do not have an equal relationship with the Father as you do. Others will misrepresent you. Some will even oppose you, and you will find yourself lonely many times. You will find yourself being the one always looking for friends to hang out with, but they will not be looking for you. God moves in stillness and in the quiet. Isaiah the prophet says, in quietness and in confidence will be your strength. Learning to be still will help us know that He is God.

When you are in spiritual training, as an ambassador of Christ, you will need an ear to hear what the Spirit is saying to YOU. There is no second hand faith, you have to do this all alone just you and the Holy Spirit. He will always point you to Jesus. As you remain in the quiet, you will start feeling a draw to spend more time with Him. Especially, in the wee hours of the morning when he wakes you up to speak to Him, and listening for His response will increase you in the spirit. The Word of God will be **on** your heart as the Scriptures say, because after He begins to break you, His Word will fall right in without being forced to enter. The Holy Spirit is a gentleman. He does not force Himself on anyone. All you have to do beloved, is make sure you are right in the sight of the Lord, by doing what He commands of you. Love Him with everything of who you are. Call out His name in the good times and the bad times. Turmoil doesn't always have to be your last name. Jesus' name is above everything imaginable in all of creation. We have music, lyrics, artistry, dance, and so much more that demonstrates our love to Him, and for Him. When you get close to the Lord and you begin to have a deeper relationship, you will learn when to speak and when not to speak. After you do all the worshipping, and praising the Lord, you will need to set an environment to have quietness and stillness to rule your home. Learning to wait on the Lord in the quiet helps us to endure through hardships and troubles. Educating yourself to have the character to be able to listen, slow to speak, and slow to become angry when these challenging issues arrive.

*In quietness and confidence shall be your strength.*
**Isaiah 30:15** *(NKJV)*

*It is good that a man should both hope and quietly wait for the salvation of the LORD.*
**Lam. 3:26** *(KJV)*

*Let every man be swift to hear, slow to speak, slow to wrath.*
**James 1:19** *(KJV)*

*Be still, and know that I am God.*
**Psalms 46:10** *(NKJV)*

## BROKEN BUT BLESSED

*Broken* means in the Webster, to be fractured, upheld, discontinuous, or interrupted. In a way this is true with God when He decides to break you, you become fractured, broken, interrupted in your everyday ways. You will be upheld by seeing situations that you are looking forward to fall into place—discontinued. Things will become dry and people start falling away from you. Slowly, but surely it *will* happen. Sometimes, it will not even come by the asking. When the Lord so chooses to interrupt you, it will come to pass. However, this mainly happens when God is calling you or training you for ministry.

Always be in a place so you could be able to listen to His voice while sensing His hearts desire for your life. He is not a toy you play with any time you become bored and uninterested. Many unbelievers in the past have tested Him and have paid a high price. The owner of the Titanic stood on the bow, cursed God and shook his fist to heaven in doubt and anger, dictating to the Lord that He couldn't sink his ship. As you very well know on the night of April 1912, a huge iceberg struck the ship and sank it, as a result of him blaspheming the Lord, as many have done in the past and still today. For year's, Christians claimed they want to change their lifestyles, ways, or their attitude, one thing they failed to realize, is if you haven't changed after all this time as He has been pricking your heart to change, it shows you are not willing to go through the fire of brokenness. You must fall on the "Rock" and become broken, rather then having the "Rock" fall on you, and become like ashes and dust. We have to learn to trust God with all our hearts, he knows how to change us and mold us. Fear is not of God, and there are many Scriptures that deal with fear. *For God has not given us a spirit of fear, but of power and of love and of a sound mind.* 2 Tim 1:7 (NKJV). Do not let the devil stop you from becoming broken and poured out, before God and man. The Book of Psalms helps you to have a relationship with God by worshipping and praising Him correctly, and the Book of Proverbs helps you to have the wisdom to deal with every day people.

The Holy Spirit is the Spirit of Christ. Christ came back to the Earth and said, "A spirit doesn't have flesh and bone like I have." Where is His Spirit? He only mentioned that He was flesh and bone. The simple answer was that His Spirit is on the Earth residing with us. This is a mystery, because the Bible says that Jesus' Spirit is not in heaven but in us. Plainly, this means He is body and bone, but not Spirit, since He sent His Spirit here.

The Lord one day told me that He brought Jesus to the Earth to show us He can be on the Earth and be in heaven all at the same time. The purpose of Him coming to die is to redeem mankind blameless without sin back to our Father. This is a humbling experience, when the Holy Ghost reveals the deep things of God. I know this may not be a huge life changing revelation, but to others it may be. This goes to show us that God is capable of doing whatever He pleases when He wants to. To know that God is omniscient, omnipresent, and omnipotent is a humbling thought. On the other hand, I encourage you to never feel scared or fear, the path of humility. Even though you and I serve an Eternal God, we know He has our back no matter what kind of mountain we face. Most times we get there through trials of fire and heartaches. Psalms states in chapter 34:18, "The Lord is close to the broken hearted." He will be by your side, and you just have to make sure that you take Him at His Word! He will perform it.

Love has humility in it. Love is not proud, Love doesn't hold a record of wrongs, Love is not jealous (1 Cor. 13:1-13). I have been guilty of these emotions before. It's not to say I do not deal with issues, I just learned to depend on God for everything that comes my way. It doesn't matter if its negative or positive, bad news or good news. The Bible says we must guard our heart and spirit. That is why I put so much emphasis in chapter one. You have to do just that, guard your spirit or the enemy will have a field day with your mind and thoughts. Not every thought that comes into your mind is yours. The main ploy of the devil is to cast fiery darts (thoughts) into your mind, to break down your faith. Counterfeit Christians, who come to you in sheep's clothing, assuredly have polyester for wool, fangs for teeth, and paws for feet. In this age we are living in, we have to be aware and watchful of the counterfeits, sometimes they are not alone. They may even be amongst a leader in a church who is not well informed of their secret insolence, impudence and trickery. My advice to you beloved is to be aware of these types of spirits in people while walking with discernment and a lowly attitude. You will always go further in the invisible when you do, manifesting into the natural for all to see Christ's Spirit radiating from you.

*Keep thy heart with all diligence; for out of it are the issues of life.*
**Prov. 4:23** *(KJV)*

*...Christ in you, the hope of glory.*
**Col. 1:27** *(NKJV)*

*...Above all, taking* **the shield of faith** *with which you will be able to quench all the* **fiery darts** *of the wicked one.*
**Eph. 6:16** *(NKJV)* Emphasis added.

*Likewise you younger people, submit yourselves to your elders. Yes, all of you be submissive to one another, and be clothed with humility, for God resists the proud, but gives grace to the humble.*
**1 Peter 5:5** *(NKJV)*

## OBEDIENCE IS THE KEY

Our thoughts in life, as "Fallen Man," have caused wars, fights, strife, gossip, discord, pain, and everything else that is evil and negative in the world. You must read, pray, worship, and praise God every chance you get. Doing these things is how I have overcome with the help of the Holy Spirit whom I have learned to love so much. Show Him that you love Him with every thing you have in your heart. Thanking Him always because He is so good. He will help you to worship when you don't know how or having trouble doing so. Just keep reaching the heart of your Father and He will help you learn to deal with the issues that come your way. This is an everyday process. It is not over until you are gone or the rapture takes place. Jesus is your friend, when you need Him to be, and I know you desire that kind of friendship. This is a sign of loving Him: Adore His commandments and obey, read His Word, meditating on it night and day regardless if you feel like it or not. Learn to call Him "Hosanna!" when things are falling apart and you do not have any money in your bank account to pay for anything. Run to Him in your troubles and run to Him when things are good. I know if you remain in Him, you will do well and accomplish many things.

In the past relatives and believers in the Body of Christ, have challenged me negatively and given me wrong information, but I learned to forgive and love every one of them regardless. Forgiveness is such a HUGE factor in the church, in this day and age we live in we can never be too careful. These trials and tests that come as a situation through people can become weary and hectic to the new believer, and they must rely on the Lord for guidance and courage. He is always with you. He said, "I will never leave you nor forsake you." As long as you do right by God and follow his commandments, this proves we love Him. His commands are not grievous or painful, because He knows when you love Him with all your heart, mind, strength, body, soul, and spirit you will do what He says. Obedience is the Key.

*For this is the love of God, that we keep his commandments: and his commandments are not grievous.*
***1 John 5:3*** *(KJV)*

*Behold, to obey is better than sacrifice, and to heed than the fat of rams.*
***1 Sam. 15:22*** *(NKJV)*

## CAST YOUR CARES

Even though some may take God's love for weakness, they have to realize He will endure so much before His judgment falls on that person. He is long suffering but nowhere it states that He will <u>stay</u> that way. There will come a time that God will bring judgment if we do not repent. He has given us the manuscript to walk in His statutes and will. His mercy endures forever; this is a reason why my soul cries out to God. His goodness is so wonderful and impeccable, not just because He is a giver of all things. It is because I have learned to love Him regardless if I am living in plenty or in want, in spite of my necessities. You and I must take that into consideration with out complaining and murmuring (Philippians 2:14). Learn to cast your cares upon the Lord because He really does care about you. Keep in mind that when you cast your cares on Him, no matter what the issue, don't take it back by worrying. This is how you take it back, by constantly speaking about it and holding on to it again after you released it. God is greater than you can ever imagine. Worrying is the absence of hope and faith. Always asking questions about how God is going to take care of it is also considered taking it back. If you continue to worry in this manner, it's a sign of doubt and in Scripture it's considered sin. He will never leave you, even though on occasion it feels like He's not around.

*Casting all your care upon Him, for He cares for you.*
**1 Peter 5:7** *(NKJV)*

*Cast your burden on the LORD, and He shall sustain you; He shall never permit the righteous to be moved.*
**Psalms 55:22** *(NKJV)*

*Let your conduct be without covetousness; be content with such things as you have. For He Himself has said,* **I will never leave you nor forsake you.**
**Heb. 13:5** *(NKJV)* Emphasis added.


## INTEGRITY: WHAT IS IT?


In church, I had Sunday friends promising that they will be there for me no matter what. We traded phone numbers and email addresses. I say Sunday friends because they were just that. Always on Sunday after service they want to know how my family and I were doing. Thinking to myself, "If you call me like I call you, you would have known how we are." Beloved, there are many examples of rejection behavior and lack of integrity in the Body of Christ. This may seem or feel insignificant, but you would be surprised how many people have left churches because no one would talk to them or say hello. I say it does affect the heart of the Image Bearer. When individuals do this on a constant basis, it tells me a lot about that person. We are always reaching out, but no one reaches back. This behavior is called a lack of Integrity. Don't misunderstand me, not all the time it's a sign of, "I really don't care," out of sight, out of mind philosophy. I just see past the artificial attitude and the church face of a synthetic spirit. No, the Lord doesn't agree with this kind of behavior, we serve the same God. Be a man of your word, and a woman of your word. If you say you are going to do something, do just that. If you are not able to act upon your word, then let the person know. Hence, an example would be if you were working for an employer, you wouldn't say, you were going into work, and then not show up. You would make sure that you call your boss and inform him, or you will not be employed very long.

Jesus wants us to be a community who holds on to our words. We all have our days of not being able to carry out what we say, and that's okay at times, but in the same instance, if you think about it, integrity is very important in the Body of Christ. We cannot say something and not mean it. We must go forward with keeping our appointments and obligations without deviating. Like I said before, if you cannot fulfill or make the appointment, call and inform them. Another illustration would be is having a child from a previous relationship, the child is anxious, excited and ready to spend time with you, and you end up not showing up. Furthermore, it will not be long before the child stops believing you. This can generate contention between you, the child, and the child's parent. Believe it or not, this kind of thinking can bring problems into a person's life as a whole, if not dealt with quickly. I hope this small example will give you that extra push to be a person of integrity.

*The righteous man walks in his integrity; His children are blessed after him.*
**Prov. 20:7** *(NKJV)*

*Better is the poor who walks in his integrity.*
**Prov. 19:1** *(NKJV)*

*The integrity of the upright will guide them.*
**Prov. 11:3** *(NKJV)*

*So he shepherded them according to the integrity of his heart, and guided them by the skillfulness of his hands.*
**Psalms 78:72** *(NKJV)*

*Judge me, O LORD; for I have walked in mine integrity: I have trusted also in the LORD; therefore I shall not slide.*
**Psalms 26:1** *(KJV)*

# I HAVE YOU ON MY MIND

According to our standards we think we know better than God, when it comes to knowing what would be better for us. When God calls you to His ministry, the pursuit begins, like I said previously. He's trying to get something to you, not take from you. There are many passages, which prove His wisdom to be able to understand His mind. His mind is beyond human comprehension to fathom. However, He has given you His Spirit to help you understand just enough of His intelligence, so you could partake of it and come into a more profound understanding. This is the God who created our minds to be able to contain 3 million years of storage! Imagine His Mind! Before your broken period visits you, pray always, especially for Him to give you the strength, grace and power of the Holy Ghost to go through it and endure. In Psalms 23, it never said, "Although I ***stay*** in the valley," but rather, "I walk ***through*** the valley…" Reader, you can make it. Jesus constantly looks after you and advocates to the Father on your behalf when you go through the valley of adversity. You are <u>never</u> alone! It is awesome to hear "I am going through something right now." Operative word, "Through." Well, praise the Lord you are going through, rather then staying and wallowing in it. Keep this in the center of your thought process, "This too shall pass."

# IS IT WORTH IT?

Is it worth it? Yes!

Believer, you will be like gold when He is done with you. "Ready and willing," will become your motto. People start to notice a change in your life and character. In the end, it is wonderful to see and experience. When you look back at your life you will say, "I cannot believe I went through that," "I endured, and I am still here." You will be better than before, much closer to the likeness of Christ. Consider the fact my brother and sister; it wasn't you but God Himself who assisted you to be a man or woman of humility. And in this humility, you will be able to stand and receive correction; with others sensing the fact you are approachable and easier to talk to. Now that you have allowed brokenness to come, He can pour out the sweet smelling oil of anointing on your spirit. Your heart of stone conforms into the heart of flesh that Christ would desire. The Holy Spirit can do His will easier without any additional obstacles against Him. You will be able to listen to God and hear others more clearly. The Lord is able to speak to you and guide you. Communication with people will become easier, as your meekness gives God glory. Meekness is power under control.

## DAD, WHERE ARE YOU?

Speaking about meekness, and being lowly was a very long process for me. I have cried and yelled with ceaseless tears to get where I am today. The pain and suffering I had to bear were agonizing and extremely lonely. Through betrayals, loneliness, let downs, beatings, bullying, my own foolishness, misery, lack of love, problems I created for myself, accusations, being molested and raped at the age of six, and homelessness for almost a year in the streets of a city in which I knew no one, with my mother and two younger brothers. It caused me to build a huge wall in my heart to prevent anyone from penetrating it and seeing the person I really was.

Periodically, my father would show up in my life. I can remember maybe three times I have seen my father. At the age of seven, twelve, and twenty-one years of age for about four to seven days at the most each time. When I was eighteen my father was unaware of the negative situations that I had to go through especially when I became homeless. Being homeless

47

caused everything to be stripped from me, until I had nothing but a thin black trench coat on my back, against negative ten-degree weather in the middle of winter. Walking and wondering everyday where was God in all of this and my natural father. In my heart of hearts I had to start all over again from scratch, since I was stripped until nothing remained. In many ways this broke me, and yet I was hard hearted, like Pharaoh. I thought to myself, not only did my natural father abandon me but my spiritual Father abandoned me also. Reality for me was not real at all, changing the course of my ways took time. A few months down the road of my misfortunes, it entered my mind, "You are not the only one going through trials of fire, testing, and hardship, there must be others weathering something similar to mine." I had to reason with myself with the fact that there are people in the world right now, who would love to trade places with me because to them, it might look and sound like nothing, compared to their difficulties. When I read the Book of Job, it really made a lot of sense to me, why he would ask God, Why? There was so much that he had to go through.

Consequently, this was not just a, 'few months thing,' or a, 'year thing,' this was my whole entire life! All of my life has been one huge trial without me seeing or experiencing an oasis. People in the world, my friends, my family, didn't understand me. All along there was a call on my life, and I didn't even know it. This was happening in the 80's and 90's. At the same time, feeling the four walls of loneliness close in on me. Wondering where was my Dad in heaven. Eventually, the Lord did show up. He would visit me ever since I was a young child in the South Bronx, New York, sleeping in my little bed. When I received that word later in my life, that Jesus was visiting me, it made a great amount of sense to the highest regard. My Daddy after all, has been there, with all the hell I had to experience. The spiritual ingredient to all of this was to forgive my parents, God, and most importantly, myself.

## PROTECTING THE ANOINTING

Saints, I ask you this question. "Have you ever had anyone in your life, come into your circle that never went through hell, like you did, try to preach to you, or tell you what to do?" If you have, welcome to Club, "I Have Gone Through Enough." Maybe you and I can get a free T-shirt. If what you just read made you smile, it was worth writing.

On a more serious note: I tell you the truth, I went through so much in my life it was ridiculous! I share this with you, I am so thankful and I know you are too, for the mercy and grace, God has shown us. "Those who love much are the ones who have been forgiven much." So what can he or she teach you? How would you be able to minister to me, when all you went through, was not being able to put gas in your car, or had a hard time trying to park closer to a stores entrance. What has God really delivered you from? Anyone who has experienced real hell with a capital "H" in their lives will give Jesus all the glory and honor for fixing their mess. Thanking Him daily for saving them. Walk vigilantly and caution yourself against spiritual leeches, they will suck you dry until every ounce of energy is absorbed until none is left.

Some believers would cling to you because they realize who you are in the Spirit and the gift that has been bestowed upon your life. Making it their goal to try to leech into the anointing, wanting the easy way in. This reminds me when a person in the past wanted to have the anointing God has put on my life, knowing full well the entire misfortune I had to suffer. I said, "So, you want this anointing," the man says, "Yeah, I want it now!" I said, "Okay, Lord, I pray that he gets molested and raped, death to visit his close friends and family members, betrayal to come his way, drown in loneliness, be misrepresented, misunderstood, a year of homelessness, days of hunger, days of thirst, no showers, get beat up, to be almost killed in a house fire, divorce, abandonment of his father, to be almost murdered after witnessing a shooting and seeing their faces living in fear they might return, I pray that he will be put in jail, be gossiped about, falsely accused and jailed, his mother to get beaten in front of him, Lord I pray that his parents would become alcoholics and drug users." He pulled away sadistically from me and said, "Whoa!" "Wait a minute!" "Apostle Luis, don't pray for some craziness like that into my life!" I said, "Sir, didn't you say you wanted my anointing? He said arrogantly, "Yes I did?" "Well sir, if you are not willing to go through these things and more the way I did, than you are not willing to pay the price that I had to pay. The Anointing of God costs! It is not free!

Be cautious of those who want what you have, and try to drain you every chance they get. Just to steal, kill, and destroy, what God has implanted deep down inside of you. Pulling on you, fishing, trying to get to know your character and motives. Stay away from the artificial and counterfeit Christians who are trying to consume you in the spirit! Please forgive me of my boldness, but this is one of the reasons why I wrote about this topic. It's dangerous in these evil times. I know some will not go through all this, just to have the anointing, but I was trying to prove a point. I hope reader; you are gracious to me, which I know you are.

*But know this, that in the last days perilous times will come:* **For men will be lovers of themselves**, *lovers of money, boasters, proud, blasphemers, disobedient to parents, unthankful, unholy, unloving, unforgiving, slanderers, without self-control, brutal, despisers of good, traitors, headstrong,* **haughty**, *lovers of pleasure rather than lovers of God,* **having a form of godliness but denying its power**. *And from such people turn away!*
**2 Tim. 3:1-9** *(NKJV)* Emphasis added.

# THE PRIDE OF LIFE

Pride in some ways can be okay to encompass, according to the way your clothes fit, or the way you look, or maybe a sense of self worth and self-esteem. Of course, you can be proud of the way you look. As long as it doesn't become into something that stinks into the nostrils of God, then it has become something else. Apparently, the Holy Scriptures, states that our God hates pride. Notice Pride has the word "ride" in it. Believe me, pride will take you for a ride to a place you do not want to go. It will not be long before you complain about wanting to get off, and most times it is too late. When a man or woman walks in the spirit of pride, you can discern the spirit, simply by being around them because the Holy Spirit tells you. If not, then just pay close attention to what kind of tree they are and the fruit they produce. Evidently, some fruit have worms in the center, so you must be very careful.

*Pride goes before destruction, and a haughty spirit before a fall. Better to be of a humble spirit with the lowly, than to divide the spoil with the proud.* **Prov. 16:18-19** *(NKJV)*

*By pride comes nothing but strife, but with the well advised is wisdom.* **Prov. 13:10** *(NKJV)*

In fact, Jesus was tempted by the devil with a question associated with the "pride of life." As I have studied the Word of the Lord, I came to know Him on a deeper, more intimate level. I see what pride and its spiritual cousins are: arrogance, conceit, pleasure, self-gratification and smugness, were doing to me and in all of my relationships. Just so you could be refreshed in your memory, before I began to perceive my "Valley of Brokenness," I had to step into my own life first, to see what others saw in me with the help of the Spirit of God. He helped me to be able to make a distinction of all the junk that was killing me on the inside, which I did not discern before. If you do not draw near to God so God can draw near to you, it will suffocate your relationships too. I tell you the truth, having vision is not the same as having sight, and this is part of being kingdom minded, which I will write about later. As you come to a conclusion of learning how to be vigilant and sober in the things of the spirit that come your way, especially in direct contact with the vision of your leaders, God will take you to different heights in the Spirit that will bring you to your knees. You will have no other choice but to fight with the Word of God. When a believer in Christ comes against this celebrated idea, strong opposition will start to go beyond you. This is what Jesus perceived from the words Satan spoke to Him about. Jesus was probably thinking to Himself, "Satan, you are such a fool. How are you going to give me something that is already mine?" Visualize this in your mind for a moment. How would I look stealing a brand new television out of your home, and then in turn try to sell it back to you? Sounds foolish don't it? Personally, that is stupidity in my mind. The devil offered Jesus' kingdoms, cities, women, houses, if you will, knowing in His mind its His already. Jesus knew, that He would not bow down to Satan, his pride and self-centered desires of impiety and malevolence.

*Again, the devil took Him up on an exceedingly high mountain, and showed Him all the kingdoms of the world and their glory. And he said to Him, "All these things I will give You if You will fall down and worship me." Then Jesus said to him, away with you, Satan! For it is written, 'you shall worship the LORD your God, and Him only you shall serve. Then the devil left Him, and behold, angels came and ministered to Him.*
**Matt. 4:8-11** *(NKJV)*

Pride is all about, "ME" and what "I" can get out of the deal. Pride destroys without the concern of others. Self-gratification in all areas of life is "his" evil fill. Friends, 'caution' should be your middle name, because pride is a spirit of "Leviathan."

Beware of that spirit, it will eradicate anyone, saved or unsaved. In the end we know the Great God Almighty will punish that impertinent spirit.

*In that day the LORD with his sore and great and strong sword shall punish* **leviathan** *the piercing serpent, even leviathan that crooked serpent...* **Isaiah 27:1** *(KJV)* Emphasis added.

*You broke the heads of* **Leviathan** *in pieces, and gave him as food to the people inhabiting the wilderness.* **Psalms 74:14** *(NKJV)* Emphasis added.

Self-importance and smugness always takes and greed's for more, constantly. Never satisfied with the now. Impatience is the cousin of pride. If you are not aware, as I said earlier, it will tear down what you hold dear. For example: if you are driving in your city and a driver is in front of you slowing you down, you keep beeping the horn, trying to get around feeling your anger rising up inside, then as you finally pass the vehicle you give them half of a peace sign that is pride combined with a spirit of anger. The Bible tells us to become angry but do not sin. Or maybe you are sitting at a traffic light and it's taking a toll on you, because its not changing fast enough. That is a sign of pride. "I want it now, I don't care about anyone else's wants, but my own!" I am not talking about, emergencies, or things of that nature. Knowingly, you didn't have to rush but you rush anyway. What happened with "Letting patience have its perfect work in you?" These are the little signs of pride in our lives, "just like the little foxes." Sometimes we try to look for the big things to see what a person deals with, we have to be prudent and wise in the spirit, letting God help us to be more like Him, to break the spirit of pride off you and out of your life.

*But let patience have its perfect work, that you may be perfect and complete, lacking nothing.*
**James 1:4** *(NKJV)*

My wife and I knew a couple who would never pray for patience, because they were afraid it will only bring lots of trouble and tribulation. That was the spirit of fear speaking to them. Jesus will never give you patience, but will allow various oppositions to work in your favor by going through storms. When those battles and conflicts come your way, it will not feel like it's training you while it is happening, but it will be working in your favor when it is finished, you will then thank God when you look back. In the end you will have the spirit of patience, to deal with an irritated or angry spouse, your terrible boss, or any difficulty that may come your way. You would be trained in the fortitude of being slow to anger, peace, love, and much more, by simply being patient.

Now that I am wiser by the grace of Almighty God, that was the wrong attitude for me to have, for the simple fact, it not only violated James 1:4 as you see above, it will also stop you from totally breaking the spirit of haughtiness, it will also refrain you from attaining a oneness of peace and meekness. Brother or sister–think about it.

## ME, MYSELF, AND I

Warning! Pride is a Spirit Killer! In the past, humility was not my strong point. I was very controlling in my marriage, children, and in the direction of others. Saints, there were times pride came and raised its ugly head, and I had to fight myself with the power of the Spirit, it's just not as bad as it used to be. The more time you spend with God and His Word, it gets better and better as the months go by. I must *always* rely on the Holy Spirit everyday to help me because I do fall short when it arises. Always seeking a way out and running to the altar in prayer and fasting to help me in my need.

Keeping this ugly spirit far as possible helps me to see clearly, so I don't have to have things my way all the time. Pride doesn't like anyone telling it what to do. You feel like you do not need any help because you have everything under control and figured out, so I thought.

Friend, did you know that pride could bring other spirits into your life if you don't deal with it immediately? Men and women have to realize that we deal with things that are in 'High and low places.' I almost destroyed my second marriage, for not being willing to just submit to my wife and respect her. I drove my first wife to a different person, because I was cold in my heart and in my thoughts. Wanting things to go through a certain direction, which was a major focus for me. My Mother didn't want me in her house. The way I spoke to her and dishonored her in more ways you can imagine was very sharp and piercing. Pride was the bed I slept on, and rebellion was my pillow, while stubbornness was my blanket. My life has been a very rough and hard path; I stepped on a lot of toes, and burned bridges with my actions and words. I would love to meet the person who said, sticks and stones break bones but words don't ever hurt. News Flash! Words hurt destroying the lives of people by the thousands. If only graves can speak.

As you read the passages of Scripture you will come to a parable about the prodigal son. I was the son that stood at home and also the other living a riotous life. Friends did not want to be around me. There were times our friends loved to hang around my wife, as long as I wasn't around. That really bothered me and hurted, knowing I was a born again Christian just like them. With all of my being I tried to figure out why others eluded me, it really boggled my mind. Seeing my behavior was so hard to grasp, part of me just didn't want to see what they saw, yearning to stay in my denial. I would read my Bible and then condemn my wife for not reading. Praying with all these sophisticated linguistical skills just to judge my wife for not speaking the same. A heart of a Pharisee and the mind of a Sadducee took a toll on her spirit. My wife, Michelle, kept it to herself for many years. She didn't want to hurt me by telling me what our friends have said about me. Blaming her would have been my primary target. First, for allowing others to talk about me wondering why they didn't confront me about the issue, instead of telling her. Now I see, looking back, I believe the spirit of anger I had would not have taken correction that easily. Several others were afraid of me also for the reason of knowing Wing Chun Kung Fu and being a Grandmaster of my own martial art system, I've studied and trained for thirty years. Wanting my own family and other brothers and sisters in the Lord to be afraid of me was not an ambition for me. In my pride Beloved, I just couldn't for the life of me realize what was going on in my soul. Writing this hurts me even now, knowing I was so hard on my wife, the kids, my mother, brothers, and friends. This was my life circle of trust with my relatives. In the meantime, all I was doing was hurting them.

I questioned God. With tears and a broken spirit, I yelled from the top of my lungs.

"Lord, who am I?"

"Tell me who I am?"

"Tell me what I can do?"

"Is this who I have become?"

"Does my life stop here?"

"What is my true identity?"

"Would I ever know my true purpose in this life?"

"Why do I keep hurting everyone who gets near me?"

"If this is who I am, I no longer want it!"

Suicidal thoughts of killing myself began to flood my mind trying to convince me that I will never change, and by taking my life, it'll stop the hurt and I will no longer be able to hurt others anymore. The trash of my past came to haunt me as these old feelings started to arise in the midst of my mind. I thought about jumping off a bridge that was near my home. Contemplating to walk in front of a truck. Besieged with evil imaginations I thought to myself,

"Maybe that would help the situation."

"My wife could marry someone who is good to her."

"My mother would be happier if I were just gone."

"Who needs me anyway, I'm a failure?"

Promises would flow from my lips, but a facial gesture of doubt was the feedback I was receiving from each person. The nights I had of tears and heartache will never leave my mind. Overwhelmed by fear that one day my wife would come home and say its over. Dreading my friends emailing me, declaring an end to their visits to our home. Mom to call and say, "you are no longer welcomed in my house." I had to run to the Lord for new breath! For new life! You have no idea what it is, if you have not yet experienced the breaking of the human spirit. Everything around me was falling apart. Crying out to God to change me hurted as well, and Him changing my change ached all the more. Wondering if there will be a light at the end of the burrow of my inner man. Then trade it for a new character and a clean heart. Although I was saved, my mentality was not renewed. I had hidden anger, bitterness, resentment, and I wanted to be compensated by everyone. Especially, from my own mother, wanting her to pay me what she had stole years before. Pay for the days of her, abandoning me and causing me to be homeless, and allowing me to be molested, even though I kept silent about it for twenty-seven years and didn't tell her. I was just not making any sense at all in my own frame of thinking. Saints, it's critically important to realize that change is possible and the Lord needs us to be broken. Paying attention to what apostle Peter said about our character toward others was not in my spirit at that time.

*Finally, all of you be of one mind, having compassion for one another; love as brothers, be tenderhearted, be courteous; not returning evil for evil or reviling for reviling, but on the contrary blessing, knowing that you were called to this, that you may inherit a blessing. For "He who would love life and see good days, let him refrain his tongue from evil, and his lips from speaking deceit. Let him turn away from evil and do good; Let him seek peace and pursue it. For the eyes of the LORD are on the righteous, and His ears are open to their prayers; but the face of the LORD is against those who do evil.*
**1 Peter 3:8-12** *(NKJV)*

## RENEWED AND ACCEPTED

When I read those words out loud, it pierced my spirit. There is so much more that happened in my life. I am sure someone out there has gone through much worse compared to what happened to me. Wishing that if this is the only thing I went through, I know someone out there would trade with me in a minute. Stories that came across my way were unbearable to take note. Wondering, "If they could survive that horrific lifestyle, than I could endure mine and make a change for the better." I assure you, my life of obedience was on a separate mantle in the spirit. Walking back into reality, with anticipation and optimism was very gloomy. I wasn't sure if anyone would give me a second chance. Challenges were manifesting in ways I couldn't even articulate with words, engulfed me. The Lord took me and honored my questions, by putting me into a blaze of transformation. Let me tell you, it is a very hot place to be in. Afterwards, with much prayer, fasting, and finally being obedient to the Lord and His Word, I was able to listen for the first time. The spirit of anger would not overtake me like it used to.

A renewed mind and heart took a charge of my motives to see my true self. My wife and I had a long talk. It was the best talk I ever had with her and the kids. An absolution was needed in that area and it had blessed me. Not knowing how much damage I've caused with that murdering prideful spirit and attitude. I went back to my mother and apologized to her with all of my soul and asked for forgiveness. Taking full responsibility for my pessimistic actions and representing it to my brothers and sisters in Christ for their exoneration. Amnesty was very much needed to all that I held dear. There is so much more to write about this, but this is written so you can believe that God can change a heart that's willing. No matter the concern or need, the Holy Spirit will run to your rescue. To be able to praise God now, with my whole heart felt and feels so good. I am no longer in bondage to those things. Everyday I wake up by the grace of God and start my day refreshed and renewed, to never look back and become that man I once was. Admitting that I sinned against my own family and friends has helped me appreciate and realize new mercies in Christ. In my own view, I would not even blame them if they did not forgive me. I praise God that they did. I had to know myself all over again, and with the help of God, the Holy Ghost came and fulfilled Himself in me still to this day. Thank you Jesus!

## DEAD MAN WALKING

Subsequently, old friends from the past would still come up to me, and try to incite and inflame the old me. With refinement and gentleness I turn them down and say sympathetically, "Sir, please don't try to resurrect a man who died a long time ago, that Luis Lopez no longer exists." The cool thing is you don't have to give them Bible passages and plead the blood, and give them this entire church program that you've changed for the better. Just something simple would suffice. If the Lord has done a perfect work in you, you will have the enemy bring people up from your past to rekindle the *old man*. Don't hesitate to say that the *old you* no longer exist. You will thank yourself later for the trouble you have just avoided, and bring Glory to God! Never take away His Glory for the change in your life. He deserves every single word of praise for it. Amen.

# CHAPTER THREE

# THE BEGINNING OF WISDOM

# Chapter Three

## THE BEGINNING OF WISDOM

*The fear of the LORD is the beginning of wisdom.*

**—Psalms 111:10**

THE FEAR OF THE LORD, in our day and age is no longer demonstrated, which is the beginning of God's holy wisdom. We are taking His commandments out of governmental and federal areas. We are telling our children in schools to stop praying. Teaching the next generation that the Bible is just a book of fairy tales and stories. One thing we have to understand, no one can ever take prayer out of schools, because when we think a prayer or even before we begin to speak, He hears us. Ironically, many Christians were taught that the devil could hear you thinking. Therefore, believers feel they shouldn't pray in their head, because they have been programmed to assume Satan knows what we are saying to God. This is funny to me since I have never found that in the pages of the Bible. Well, Good News Saints! Your God is the only one that can hear and see your heart and mind thinking!

*Then hear thou in heaven thy dwelling place, and forgive, and do, and give to every man according to his ways,* **whose heart thou knowest; for thou, even thou only, knowest the hearts of all the children of men.**
**1 Kings 8:39** *(KJV)* Emphasis added.

*And the Spirit of the LORD fell upon me, and said unto me, Speak; Thus saith the LORD; Thus have ye said, O house of Israel:* **for I know the things that come into your mind, every one of them.**
**Ezekiel 11:5** *(KJV)* Emphasis added.

*For there is not a word in my tongue, but, lo, O LORD, thou knowest it altogether.*
**Psalms 139:4** *(KJV)*

From Gen. 9:2 to Rev. 19:5, you will find the word "Fear" appearing in the Bible four hundred times, with different meanings, interpretations and connotations. The most important is the fear of the Lord, knowing full well we don't have to fear or fear praying anywhere according to the Word of our God. The beginning of wisdom will help you stay in position where you need to be and also put things in its proper angle. In order to categorize ourselves to be in a place of respect and honor toward the Lord, we have to embrace His Word daily. Here are three similar passages to heighten His point of view.

*My son, if you receive my words, And treasure my commands within you, so that you incline your ear to wisdom, and apply your heart to understanding; Yes, if you cry out for discernment, And lift up your voice for understanding, If you seek her as silver, And search for her as* for *hidden treasures; Then you will understand* **the fear of the LORD,** *and find the knowledge of God.*
**Prov. 2:1-5** *(NKJV)* Emphasis added.

*If My people who are called by My name will humble themselves, and pray and seek My face, and turn from their wicked ways, then I will hear from heaven, and will forgive their sin and heal their land.*
**2 Chron. 7:14** *(NKJV)*

*...If you walk in My statutes, execute My judgments, keep all My commandments, and walk in them, then I will perform My word with you...*
**1 Kings 6:12** *(NKJV)*

Meditate on this for a moment. If a person doesn't fear God, whether they are Christian or a sinner, they will never come to an apex of total life, and that total life is only by following the narrow steps of repentance and obedience Jesus outlined for all of us.

Why would anyone listen to a God who commands all people everywhere to follow His statutes, His footsteps, if there is no fear? Why? In their minds their are no limits, fear of God, or warning signs of consequence. *Fear,* and the Lord to them is only a byword of false hopes and no perpetuity after you pass away. Most have been taught and believe we are like plain animals, just here to live, work, and die and go into a 'no consciousness' sleep and transported into an epoch without end. These evil philosophies have no solid foundation to congeal real truth and hard facts of real conformity. Fearing God helps you keep track so you don't have to keep falling into the snares of Satan's schemes. Be inspired to know that the Holy Spirit will always be there for you to assist and sanction you into newness of living, at the same time defend you when the flood waters of dissension tries to step over your boundaries.

# WARNING: REPENT AND BE RESTORED

Unfortunately, many leaders today are not listening with the heart of fear toward God in these last days. The Spirit of God is not taken seriously, but for a joke. Too many people saying they are on the side of the Lord, but all they are transmitting is a distorted outlook into the church, with the indication of a 'Jezebel', and a 'Judas Iscariot' spirit. Like I have been saying through out the pages of this book. Be aware of the enemy! Know what your true purpose is in your life. If not, your 'Greatness' within your belly will die and never be manifested again! Time is drawing near and the judgment to all people is closer than it has ever been. I plead with you to take this walk very seriously and get right in the sight of the Lord. In the words of John the Baptist, "Repent! For His Kingdom draws near!" This is not a game to be toying with; this is your life, especially if you are a leader or a minister of the Gospel, if they fall their punishment in hell is much greater than that who knows less than you and a lower position in the spirit, the Bible says. Hear me, the grace of God is being trampled underfoot and His mercy is being taken advantage of. His Spirit will strive with man for so long. We all must be reminded that it is a terrible thing to fall into the hands of the Living God! Lets not take the Lord for granted. We must repent everywhere we are about to meet the King. Whether in death or the catching away, we still must repent no matter the circumstances, fighting and repelling from being marginalized; restored back to Him and His everlasting love affair!

# THE OTHER SIDE OF GOD

This is your Father, my Father. When are we going to show Him through our lives we truly do love Him? Fear God! Ultimately, you will give an account to Him one day soon, and you do not want to be left behind, or worse, enter into the resurrection of the wicked dead. Your soul and spirit are going to stand in front of Christ. Every soul and spirit from every man, woman, and child will never die for the reason it is eternal and never physically die as we know death, but it will suffer in hell, which is considered a second death of the spirit. We will live forever because anything that comes out of the mouth of God is eternal. It's up to you to choose while you are alive in this world where you want to spend eternity.

The reason why He sends those who evade His Son to hell is because there is nowhere else to send them, but into an eternal torment and total separation from the Master of creation. I plead with so many in the ministry to get it right and stop dabbling with sin, and they consider me to be too spiritual or too righteous. I respond that you can never be spiritual enough. Doesn't the Word say in the New Testament to walk after the Spirit and not the flesh? Can we say that we are ready to stand before Him, if He came now, for us? Or, will you barely make it? You have to have a diligent spirit to do the work God has set before you. Your works will turn into hay and stubble if genuine love is not portrayed in the spirit and soul of the believer. Again, we must walk after the Spirit, and yes, you and I fall short and mess up as I explained, but at the same time we must recognize how we are behaving so we do not stay where Satan and the flesh wants us.

*If his work is burned up, he will suffer {the loss}. However, **he will be saved, though it will be like going through a fire**.*
**1 Cor. 3:15** *(Gods Word)* Emphasis added.

Brothers and sisters we need to make sure, God is pleased with us. I desire to hear, "Well done my good and faithful servant." Knowing that "God is love" and the love that He gives echoes throughout the pages of the Bible, for you and I to understand where His heart is. Dare to be relentless with the things of God. Our reward is coming for all the concerns we had to face while on this earth. The human race has to understand that God is head over heels in love with us. Barely making it and not putting our entire heart and mind to serving Him will not work. I tell you the truth, Saints, that is not going to do it if we don't get it together. I know you have it in you to do it. Don't wait until Judgment Day to get here before you decide to make a change for the better. If you do, it will be too late! His judgments are swift and very sudden. If the *waiting* has come to full fruition and you were caught in the act of rebellion and no repentance, He said He would have you depart from His presence and spew you out of His mouth. I implore you to put into operation a lifestyle of holiness and reverence into action now, thus, His hand of ballast will not have to weigh you down and press you into the center of the earth. You can't live like God in public, and act like the devil at home. You must be striving for Godliness all the time, especially when you are alone, this shows the Lord and yourself, your true character and where you are in your spirit. Too much has been arising internally in the churches behind closed doors. Jesus is looking for a house, a temple, without spot or blemish, or He will leave you behind. Anyone who is reading this, don't take it lightly, there are enough counterfeits calling themselves Christians as it is, please don't be one more added to this list of artificiality. Be on fire for God or cold for God, don't mingle in between, it will anger the Lord in a very somber manner.

*So then, because you are lukewarm, and neither cold nor hot, I will vomit you out of My mouth.*
**Rev. 3:16** *(NKJV)*

*And then will I profess unto them, I never knew you: depart from me, ye that work iniquity.*
**Matt. 7:23** *(KJV)*

Spiritual roll models will elevate you drastically, in rectitude from the eye view of heaven. Comprehending the fact that we cannot be over righteous and overly wicked. Solomon made it very clear in his writings to the people of his day about walking on this destructive path. Knowing the outcome of specific behaviors that were familiar to Solomon in his wisdom, I believe he had candidates, if you will, who anticipated a solution to certain problems. The end result disintegrated before his eyes; because the individual thought they had it all under their control, with being above and beyond their means of spiritual matters greater than Solomon's wisdom.

*Do not be overly righteous, nor be overly wise: Why should you destroy yourself? Do not be overly wicked, nor be foolish: Why should you die before your time?*
**Eccl. 7:16-17** *(NKJV)*

## WHICH ONE WILL YOU CHOOSE?

A garment of salvation is different than a robe of righteousness (Isa. 61:10). Which one will you choose, the garment or the robe? You must put on the Lord Jesus Christ no matter what circumstances come your way. God desires to be first in our lives, before children, spouses, our jobs, and material things. Jesus has to be number one at all times. It is possible to put Him first. "All things are possible for those who believe." Saints, we must get used to the fact that we have to **listen** to the prompting and voice of the Holy Spirit. God wants us to have reverential fear directed to Him. Not as the world knows fear but the way the Bible explains it. A large number of people who profess they love God, do not follow His sayings. Basically, not everyone who professes Christ is right with the Lord.

Notice what James says, "Be a doer of the Word and not a hearer only deceiving yourself." We cannot just praise the Lord with our lips honoring God in public and living a lie and being disobedient behind closed doors too. There is a lot of that going on already and that is a perfect example of a counterfeit Christian. Portraying in the limelight you are this holy and anointed saint of God, and yet, while no one is watching you, living like Satan. Loving God is an act of relational prayership. I understand that God is invisible, but we must spend time with Him just like we do with people with honesty and integrity in the sight of God and all men. We are promised in Scripture and the few I provided you from Proverbs, that if we fear God and Love Him and be obedient, we would live longer lives, and become whole. Now ask your self this, which will you choose? A Garment or a Robe? What's the difference you ask? The Garment takes you longer to get to God walking with total and complete obedience and the Robe does not, you have straight access!

*Hear, my son, and receive my sayings, and **the years of your life will be many**. I have taught you in the way of wisdom; I have led you in right paths. When you walk, your steps will not be hindered, and when you run, you will not stumble. Take firm hold of instruction, do not let go; Keep her, for she is your life.*
***Prov. 4:10-13*** *(NKJV)* Emphasis added.

He will satisfy the thirsty and give strength to the weary. The problem I see with kids, teenagers, and young adults they don't even fear their parents they do see, let alone God who they don't see. The Christ in us the Hope of Glory can train them in the way they should go and when they get older, they will not depart from it. It also suits the unrighteous as well. Training up a child in the way he or she should go, in wickedness, he or she will not depart from that. It's not in all cases but in several. Pay close attention Saints in what God is saying to you in the church and outside of church and in your homes. The whole duty of man is to Fear God and follow hard after Him, and obey His Word. Jesus is that Word!

*Let us hear the conclusion of the whole matter:* **Fear God,** *and keep his commandments: for* **this is the whole duty of man.**
**Eccl. 12:13** *(KJV)* Emphasis added.

## KNOWN BY ASSOCIATION

You must associate with people who are powerful in the Lord. It's good for you to provoke wisdom and knowledge when the anointing is available. Surround yourself with those who bear good and lasting fruit, fruit takes time to grow on a tree and expand, as well as developing seeds. In obedience you will do the same, let time pass so the seed can grow in you as a tree of maturity, and allow it to expand and come into the character of being that 'Total Man' or 'Woman' of Christ you were called to be, from the foundations of the world. This means you have been obedient and diligent with the Spirit of The Holy, and have produced seed to plant into His kingdom in order to reap a harvest of your righteousness in Christ. This is not a sprint race but a relay. The race of faith is not given to the swift but to the diligent. We hand the baton of God's Word brother-to-brother and sister-to-sister, to encourage, edify, exhort, rebuke, and correct in love. Just like the Apostles and Prophets did before us and still to this day initiate, by the authority of the Most High, instructing when they should prophesy or bring forth the Word. Believers need to honor the wisdom and understanding when these ministers bring forth revelation to the church body. Giving heed to these ministers and the gifts that obtrudes of the anointing must be recognized and respected. Christians will begin to become sensitive to the requests and requirements of what is needed to perform in the right season with the leading of the Spirit. Furthermore, I am astonished and amazed how much we have veered off from showing the respect that the ministers of God deserves, since reverence has not entered into the mind and spirit of the believer. Reverential fear of the Lord is slowly dissipating, slowly vanishing, as well in the direction of the anointed people He ordains. Beloved, you must get in position to bring into culmination what Christ has for you, most of the time the Lord uses His ministers to do so. Don't give up on yourself and those whom the Spirit of Christ has put in position. Re-think very carefully where God is coming from as He anoints the chosen and leads them into a higher dimension of ministry and power. Do not violate this Scripture, and if you are the one being victimized with pure foolishness, pray and warn them with what the prophet David said.

*He permitted no one to do them wrong; Yes, He rebuked kings for their sakes, saying, "Do not touch My anointed ones, and do My prophets no harm."*
**Psalms 105:14-15** *(NKJV)*


## PICK A SIDE AND COMPLY


Christians need to come under the hand of The Almighty and learn to build a solid foundation of respectability and sanctity, in order to have fullness of life, wholeness, with nothing missing, or broken. Intermittently, things might not feel or give the impression that our Saviors presence or hand is accessible to you, causing you to think that God is not real at times, but this is all deception from our flesh with the devil intensifying what we already conjured up in the blueprint of our thoughts. Quote and read His Word daily, this is what puts us back into alignment with the Lord. One key element is prayer, which helps you to get closer to God, because once you recognize that the reality of God is through revelation and relationship, it will pervade and encompass you in and enter the Lord's presence, with love and expectancy into holy fear, which in turn gives the Lord true worship. I always like to remind anyone that God is a good God, he loves you and your family more then you could or would ever anticipate. Remember, in this realm we call the earth, prayer is your lifeline of liberty and potency from this place to that place we call "mi casa," our home, which is heaven.

## ABOVE YOUR STANDARDS

It has not entered into our hearts and minds how much the Savior really loves us (See 1 Cor. 2:9 & Isa. 64:4). When you demonstrate to God that He is number one in complete totality of your being, in the same liberty show others that He is number one in your life. Unequivocally, His blessings will begin to fall on you, and where ever you go He will be there. His presence as the trinity–Father, Son, and Holy Spirit will simply overtake you. Dispatching angels to guard you all the days you have on earth, working and performing for the body of believers and those who are in desperate need to hear a Word of hope. The New Testament expresses, "men should always pray, and pray always without ceasing." Never giving up hope, having faith and believing what has been spoken. You will reap quickly; payday will be here soon! Meditate and ponder these questions.

"How can we go on sinning, and not repent?"

"How can we say, we fear God and then do the opposite knowing full well it is contrary to Him and His will?"

"Why do we always have to break Yahweh's heart?"

> We dishonor Him and hurt His feelings. We must stop! We cant live a lifestyle of disobedience when the winds of rejection and trials start to overtake us. The real question is,

"What are you going to do about it?"

"Are you going to stand firm through the pain and distress?"

"What makes me better than God that I can't go through anything also?"

Jesus, the Son of God had to undergo the pain and agony of rejection, torment, betrayal, and all different kinds of horrific events that took residence in His life. It pleased the Lord God to bring this judgment on His Son understanding in His infinite wisdom what it will do for countless millions in the future, and probably billions. Oh, if we only knew what is coming for the born again saint, if he or she stay committed, centered, and focused when the Day of Christ arrives, it's going to be captivating. Unmistakably, for mankind to actually experience what's to come, a light must come on in the inside of that believer to listen and comply what was instructed. Obey the Spirit of God when He speaks to you, to the best of your ability. If not, a price will be paid as you continue to disprove what has been set before you. It will cost you all of eternity. Do not get curious to see what's on the other side of the valley of judgment, it is not appealing. His punishments are great because He is Great. His love is great because He is Great. His thoughts are not your thoughts, and His ways are not your ways, since He is Great.

*For My thoughts are not your thoughts, nor are your ways My ways, says the LORD. For as the heavens are higher than the earth, so are My ways higher than your ways, and My thoughts than your thoughts.*
**Isaiah 55:8-9** *(NKJV)*

Visualize for a moment a Christian who is about, let's say, six feet tall. That is as high as he would think compared to the Lord's mental capacity. God thinks on an omni-dimensional mental level, beyond mankind's aptitude. Scientists and doctors who study the brain say in our day we use 10 to 12 percent of our brain cells, in comparison with Albert Einstein who was considered the smartest man in the world in his time, using 18 percent of his brain cell. Hence, creating E=mc2 leading to the development of the atomic bomb. As distinguished as he was, his brain capacity was no match with Noah's, which is believed the antediluvian people of his day used both halves of their brain, considering 100 percent brain cell activity. In my thesis, my Bible tells me "the man Christ Jesus" is still greater than any man can ever display, since it was because of Christ giving us that kind of knowledge. All things come together to bring satisfaction in knowing He is in control of the "Everyday Man," no matter how great he might be in the eyes of mankind.

Besides the talks of knowledge and how much we know as humans, my prayer for you is that you will continue to walk in the solicitude of God vehemently like never before, causing the angels of the Lord to work on your behalf to bring prosperity, hope, deliverance, and healing into you and your families life, right now in the name of Jesus!

*Beloved, I pray that you may prosper in all things and be in health, just as your soul prospers*
**3 John 1:2** *(NKJV)*

Keep this in mind. This doctrine we put our faith in, with the people of God, sounds immense to an abundant amount of people. In the same consensus, we must follow the first principle in order for us to maintain the blessings of God, and that is "walking in the fear of the Lord."

*But seek first the kingdom of God and His righteousness, and all these things shall be added to you.*
**Matt. 6:33** *(NKJV)*

## HONOR YOUR FATHER AND MOTHER

Obeying your parents with reverential fear is not a horrific or devilish fear, but a deferential fear that you release out of high respect for your mother and father. Considering you recognize their authority over you, with a heart flooded with honor toward them. Thinking about my own mother helps me to realize and appreciate all that she had to put up with when it came to me. She knew giving birth to me at a young age was a choice she had to really ponder, considering the position she was already in. She had the choice to have me aborted, knowing full well her days were going to be very hard and strenuous. Residing in Brooklyn, in the toughest neighborhoods of New York City, was not a walk in the park for her. I give my mother the utmost respect, for choosing life. Although, I am climbing into my upper thirties, I praise God for the choice she made to keep me, or this vision adjacent to the others God has given me, would have never come into being. She has moments in her life where she still treats me as if I were a little kid, I know now it's because she really loves me, and in her eyes I will always be her little boy. But back in my earlier years, that would had been a problem for me feeling like her little boy, I learned to humble myself right down, since she has all the right to feel and see me in that way. Why I say that? My pride wouldn't let me see the love of a mother to a son, until I had children of my own. Like the old saying goes, "if I knew then what I know now," I would not have given my mother the lip and back talk with a great deal of disrespect. Sharply, I would respond saying, "I am man, stop treating me like a little kid, you can't talk to me that way!" In the eye of my mind, something so small and obscure was so big to me at the time; the understanding was not resonating in my heart. Issues like this were such a big deal to me, and yet so small to everyone else that I knew. Constantly overreacting about small matters, telling my friends, "my mother shouldn't treat me like that because I am a man, I'm not a little kid anymore." Indeed, this attitude I had was a mind of a child. Being shrewd with my mother was my middle name, instead of just following the commandment of honoring her while living under her roof. In my heart I wanted her to compensate me, for all the wrong she has done. A door of rebellion from my part was open, not knowing what was the final result. Due to this attitude of witchcraft, my actions worsened like she never seen before.

One day, coming over for dinner, I said some harsh things to my mom, and for the first time in my life I saw the pain of my mother's heart as she began to cry. That was the first time I really noticed her being broken, and I repented and left her home. I asked myself, "What is the matter with you?" Then I heard a small voice, "One of these days your mother will be silent and never speak again until the Last Day, so take advantage of loving her with all you have now while she is still borrowing My Breath of Lives." Ever since, that experience and repenting before the Lord camping in the broken place, now our relationship is better, thank God, since I didn't realize then what I realize now. When I heard those words something inside of me exploded, and caused me to think for the better, I encourage you to do the same. Give honor where honor is do, obey your father and mother you will live long on earth, it's a promise.

*Honor your father and your mother, that your days may be long upon the land which the LORD your God is giving you.*
**Ex. 20:12** *(NKJV)*

*Honor your father and your mother, as the LORD your God has commanded you, that your days may be long, and that it may be well with you in the land which the LORD your God is giving you.*
**Deut. 5:16** *(NKJV)*

Its true, you only have one mother, and one father, its just the 'father thing' is not as accredited like the mother's are. In the eyes of God, He doesn't see male or female, Jew or Gentile, but His children whom He loves dearly. Beloved, I am sure you must feel the same way about the love you must have with mom and dad when it comes to relationship. One day they will not be here, and we have to pick up from the legacy they leave behind. Giving us the tools to be better than they were for the Glory of God. Saints, as I said earlier, lets give honor where honor is due to our parents or parent if single. Maybe you don't have your real parents, it makes no difference to the Lord, even the one raising you is your parent. Love them with all the love and compassion you have, and illustrate how you truly feel toward them from within you. Maybe it's been awhile, or there is something between you guys that is floating above your head. Life is too short to harbor any bitterness or resentment for the past mistakes between you and your loved ones. Me, I would say to my mother since my father hasn't been around, *"Mom, you are both my mother and father, and you're my closest friend, confidant, counselor, a well of wisdom, and a powerful woman of God, I love you."*

My point is, we can assist and decipher that fearing God has been incubated in the womb of mankind, to have reverential fear for those in authority, and with this understanding if you fear the Lord, you will have the respect and fear toward many who have rule over you.

Demonstrate your love by honoring your parents for this is right. No one can take that away from you, ever. Times will come when you will not agree or get along with your parents, just keep in the back of your mind, that mom and dad love you and under it all, its really concern and care that is being depicted. Here's a secret, Friends, agree to disagree. Just because you are right doesn't mean you always have to be. To be honest, its good to just keep silent. If one evening you are at your folks house, and a spat arises and you happen to be right about something, saying what's right in a wrong way will still make you wrong. There were times my mother and I didn't get along or agree on anything. Years have gone by which I could never get back, not speaking to each other simply bickering and picking on each other. I honor God, because when the valley of brokenness and calamity decided to leave from the front doorsteps of my heart, I could say right now, that our relationship is so much better than ever before. Additionally, keep in heart the fact that this is the same admiration, devotion, understanding, fear, and love we must have directed to the Holy Spirit of God. Take time right now and give thanks to the Lord for all He has done so far in your life.

*"Thank you so much Lord for what you have done, there are no words to express what stirs in the depths of my soul."*

## THE BEGINNING OF FEAR

When the discipline of God's charge falls into your spirit, it tends to well deep and thorough, leaving no residue behind to allow the same issue to occur again. Months will go by, wondering where the Lord has been hiding in your trial of adversity. Prophet Isaiah believed, that the Lord is a God who hides Himself. Surely I looked for my Savior during all those times of misery and suffering, with my hands wide open I wondered:

"Do I really love God?"

"Am I wise enough to make sure the responsibility as a man of God is of good character?"

"Do I fear God as I should?"

Bombarded with questions, views, and images of wonderment, I prayed telling the Lord,

"How can this happen to me?"

"I fear You, but am I doing good in your eyes Lord?"

All along I was convincing myself to have Jesus see a different side of me. In actuality, I did not fear Him, as I should have. The fear of the Lord puts you in a position to help you not fall away from God when troubles come. You are reminded if you do this sin, or continue in that error of wickedness you will perish! I have total reverent fear toward the Lord. I respect who He is, and thrive for perfection. The Bible tells us that we are to seek perfection, and this will bring a spirit of excellence and completion, baptizing us into maturity and wholeness in His Son. "Perfect" means to be whole, mature, and complete; the world has perverted this word to mean: Never to think, say, or do anything wrong. That is not the case in this matter, because when the Scriptures mention this word, *perfect*, it's not to mean infallible; only Christ walked in infallibility. In essence, we must walk in perfection and faith believing that there is nothing greater than having eternal life, even though you might go through some hard trepidation, temptations, heartaches, and heavy burdens. Realize that The Comforter is always by your side. Fear the Lord, do what is right in His sight, and never mind the rest. You will live longer and Jesus will come to your aid.

*The fear of the LORD prolongs days, but the years of the wicked will be shortened.*
**Prov. 10:27** *(NKJV)*

*Come to Me, all you who labor and are heavy laden, and I will give you rest. Take My yoke upon you and learn from Me, for I am gentle and lowly in heart, and you will find rest for your souls. For My yoke is easy and My burden is light."*
**Matt. 11:28-30** *(NKJV)*

## PRAYER FOR THE WISDOM OF FEARING GOD

Father I thank you for your grace and mercy you have shown me through out my entire life. I know there isn't a way to pay you back for all you have done for me, but to give my life to you and walk in the realm of obedience. Forgive me if I have done or said anything unknowingly that upset you or dishonored you. I ask you to forgive me Lord. I realize that the fear of the Lord is the Wisdom of Christ, and very important for me to abide by your standards. I pray the Holy Spirit will retrain my mind to understand that I must give you total and true reverence, and be sincere and honest with myself to be able to come before you with humility and meekness in my spirit. I surrender my will, my ways, to you my God. Help me as I pray this new petition so you can be glorified in front of all people. From now on true worship and true praise will continue to be part of who I am, not just in public but also in secret and you will reward me openly. Thank you Father, I pray this in the name of your precious Son Jesus. Amen.

# WHO DO YOU SAY, THAT I AM?

# Chapter Four

---

# WHO DO YOU
## SAY THAT I AM?

*He said to them, "But who do you say that I am?"*
*Peter answered and said, "The Christ of God."*

**—Luke 9:20**

A NUMEROUS AMOUNT OF PEOPLE in the church need a clearer understanding concerning the five-fold ministry. The other day I met a woman that had no idea what an apostle or a prophet was or does for the Body of believers. She has been serving the Lord almost all her life; she was in her sixties, absolutely clueless. Unfortunately, many believe that apostles, and prophets do not exist today. Theologians claim, that there were no more apostles after the original twelve, because they literally walked with Christ on earth and already established the church. One loophole I found in that theory, is the fact that Paul, Barnabas, and countless others didn't walk with Christ and were considered apostles. A good amount of people that I have known throughout the years have tried to dictate to God who we are, instead of allowing the Holy Ghost to make that decision. If the Lord called you to be a prophet, lets say; and then the Spirit confirmed it through His minister(s), whether it is an apostle, or a pastor, you are to receive and walk in that call—with wisdom. You would go through whatever is needed in order to walk in that anointing, under the spiritual guidance of your pastor or whoever is above you in authority of the Spirit.

Now after a second, or a third confirmation, just to make sure we are hearing right, that is okay. It's when you start seeking more confirmation or searching for validation, this is when it becomes a problem, because now it is considered doubt and unbelief. Now others heard the Call and took it and ran with it. They go in search of a robe at their local Christian store, begin to look for a building and go full force into the ministry, not being sent yet by the Lord. This too is dangerous. Keep in mind, even "The Great Apostle," Jesus Christ was pointed out by the "Chief Prophet," John the Baptist; He too had to wait until the Father said when to go and the prophet to point Him out as the Lamb of God who takes away the world's sin. He avowed the Lord when He was coming into the water to be baptized by John to fulfill all righteousness, preparing the way for the Son of God. They were always led by the Spirit, and knew exactly what there mission was and who they were in God.

## IS IT DISOBEDIENCE?

When a man or woman of God tells an individual, by divine revelation, God has this specific calling on your life, its disobedience if that person does not receive that Word—they doubt and do not believe His Word. "How is that doubting and unbelief?" By not accepting it. We refuse and walk the other way like Jonah did to Nineveh (See Romans 8:28). You have to know who you are, Satan knows you very well and all of your likes and dislikes and weaknesses. He will make sure you do not walk in that calling and reject the prophetic Word spoken over you, misguiding the truth of who you are in the natural and in the spiritual realm. In the ordinary dimensions of the world, when you don't accept the assignment given to you, Satan will raise 'hell agents' and 'counterfeits' to commence all kinds of dissimilar things, causing confusion and turmoil.

*For God is not the author of confusion but of peace, as in all the churches of the saints.*
**1 Cor. 14:33** *(NKJV)*

## LET HIM STEAL NO MORE

Jesus asked His disciples, "Who do you say, that I AM?" By the power of the Spirit of the Lord, Peter the apostle said, "You are the Christ, the Son of the living God." Its very important beloved that you know who you are at all times, and whose you are. Subsequently, you will be able to walk in the fullness of God's power without any shadow of a doubt. Knowing who you are will bring such mayhem into the camp of the enemy it will make his head spin. Saints, he is a powerful enemy! Do not play with Satan at all whatsoever, under any circumstance. We know that the Spirit of Christ indwells us, but that is not reason enough to go ahead and become the Lone Ranger trying to take the devil on alone, just to cry out for Tanto to help and he isn't their. It is vital, Christian, and very important that you actually get this deep down into your spirit, and let it stay their. The devil's job is to try to stop you from walking right into your Call. To impede you from accepting the whisper of the Lord's voice and keep you moving the opposite direction. I advise you Saints, don't miss your Glory. That will be a terrible thing to miss the Call God has for your life, into such a greater scale, it will make your world shudder.

## THE DEVIL'S RUNWAY

Regrettably, a lot of Christians shockingly run away from the ministry, when in essence it's really God whom they are running from. Some simply just don't care to be part of the work that needs to be done. Elohim said, "The harvest is plentiful, but the workers are few." We have to get on the ball before time is up. Its sin when God is calling you into the ministry and you do not pursue it. Disobedience is not the will of God in our sphere of influence. As the Body of the Lord we must be mature enough to understand, that we need to reconsider and re-evaluate the vision. I notice that the real people of the Lord refuse, and the counterfeits are willing to go forth. Especially, by two's every single weekend in the early mornings when you are still sleeping. That is quite comical to me. Us, believers have the real truth, keeping it behind the four walls of our homes and churches. While the devil is out there in all types of weather walking in two's preaching a lie, most of them are insistent. Envision for a moment, if they were like this for Christ Jesus, they would be able to move mountains! Lets get a move on and lets stop the devil and his hell agents dead in their tracks. Get him off the runway that leads into your spirit! I speak to all evangelists to arise and go forth, we need you now more than ever! It is **always** God's will for us to preach and teach the good news to all people, in season and out of season.

## BEAUTIFUL BUT DEADLY

One night around 10:00pm, I was in my bedroom watching Christian television at home, and a famous celebrity preacher was speaking about the Holy Spirit. After the program ended, I shut the light off and went to sleep. It's hard to say when my dream actually began, but unexpectedly there were two paths about twenty feet from me. One path was on my far left, and the other directly in front of me where I was standing. It was kind of weird at first but the wide road had the sun shining high in the sky. The clouds were full and the heavens were blue and beautiful. Birds were chirping and singing, people were laughing as they leisurely walked on the road and others were playing. Married couples were having picnics on the grass near this beautiful road on each side. Strange as it may sound in my peripheral vision, this narrow path kept trying to have me re-focus, like it was calling me. There were a select few that would go into the narrow pathway, while others succumbed to take the wide road instead.

Now this narrow path was very dirty, and unpaved. There were huge weeds, roots, and large leaves like a jungle would have. In my mind I knew it would take a lot of effort to try to get through that path. It had trees and bushes knitted together that would dull a machete in minutes. I would say it needed a landscape company to come and trim the hedges, because it was in really bad shape. Essentially, the road in front of me was captivating, and I tried to veer my eyes off that narrow path. As I strolled on the fine-looking path, it turned to gold. Each brick was paved in stunning gold ingots. On each side was beautiful green grass where people were having a cookout and having family activities. Distraction settled when I looked down the road, and as far as the eye can see, it had soaring buildings, which appeared to be like an Emerald City of some sort. To my knowledge I remember the bricks were made out of all different kinds of jewels and gems.

Unexpectedly, hundreds and then thousands of people started to walk from behind me covering this wide road I was on, and eventually bumping me to pass, for the reason that they wanted to get to the City. Literally thousands were like going nuts, almost knocking others down just to get to those skyscrapers. As the road began to clear, the thought of the narrow path kept popping in and out of my head. Like I was missing something, feeling a void of emptiness in my spirit. No longer paying attention to the narrow path for the reason of being distracted by a figure, which appeared on the right hand side of the road in the distance. As I wandered and strolled looking around engaging the beauty with my eyes, and seeing families on each end of this road having a good time talking and laughing with their spouse, this figure was becoming closer and taller at the same time. When this man or some kind of figure came into focus, at about one hundred feet I started backing up, but it kept coming closer at a high level speed, then it was fifty feet, then twenty feet from me, "run for your life," were the thoughts rambling in my head. It was a burned demon general about thirteen feet tall, with its flesh exposed and his hand extended with flesh falling off his fingers, telling me in a scoffing, impious, and unbelieving manner to come to him in a dark voice:

He said, "Hmph! Come Luis, this is the wide road that leads to the good life, did you notice the other path?"

(*Sneering*) He says, "The other path is terrible looking, its not as fine-looking as this one?"

He continued,

"You will be wasting your time going through all the trouble trying to walk through that extreme narrow path, when my road is easy to travel on and so attractive, what do you say, Luuuiiissssss?"

Before I was given the opportunity to answer him, I awoke from the dream. Adjusting myself to grasp the spiritual figurative of the dream, Jesus showed me in Scripture the next morning about the narrow path that leads to life and the few who find it. Having the obedience with His will to walk in the course of it brings immortality, in contrast, to them who walk on the wide road that leads to death and destruction. I say believe God to help you choose and stay the course on the narrow path that leads to life eternal.

**Enter by the narrow gate**; *for wide is the gate and* **broad is the way that leads to destruction,** *and there are many who go in by it. Because narrow is the gate and difficult is the way which leads to life, and there are few who find it.*
**Matt. 7:13-14** *(NKJV)* Emphasis added.

## FIGHT TO THE FINISH

Sorry to say, I understand what it is to hear the Call of God, and then run away from it, because it was to heavy for me at that time. When you have a call of an Apostle, all hell turns to you. Demons know the power of the office of apostle. They do everything and anything to stop them from coming forth. But I see a mighty river visitation coming! Hallelujah to God Almighty! There is nothing Satan can do to you or me, as long as you keep your heart into the hands of the Christ of Heaven. The Spirit of God will empower you like you have never witnessed before. Stay in constant prayer.

Take into account, that it's not the position of your body, but the position of your heart. However, praying on your knees is a sign of humility, so is a person who cries out to God in need of help, standing up. Basically, you can pray anywhere, particularly those who pray from the heart then just speaking words in vain from your head. God is more concerned of heartfelt prayers than mental words of babble.

*Then He spoke a parable to them that* **men always ought to pray** *and not lose heart.*
**Luke 18:1** *(NKJV)* Emphasis added.

*Pray without ceasing.*
**1 Thess. 5:17** *(KJV)*

**Fight the good fight of faith**, *lay hold on eternal life,* **whereunto thou art also called**.
**1 Tim. 6:12** *(KJV)* Emphasis added.

During the praying and receiving the plan God has for me, the devil fought and declared war against me. Antagonizing me to the point I couldn't even think straight until the Lord intervened. It's one thing when you have an adversary, who is unyielding, using his children to come against you, then dealing with yourself on a moment-to-moment origin. It got so bad, that Satan literally had to show up. I will share that with you in a later chapter, it was a terrible experience.

## KNOW WHO YOU ARE

The Lord asked the disciples in the garden of Gethsemane, if they could stay up for one hour at least, to pray. Pastors have a very hard time getting lay members and other times the leaders to meet into the house of God to pray. Spending time with our 'Daddy' to make sure our lives are right in the sight of heaven is very important for all who are born again. Moses, Jeremiah, Joshua, and Gideon are the select few I am writing about, in regards of them believing the Lord. Joshua needed to be strong and courageous, Moses stammered, Jeremiah doubted, Gideon wondered if it was really God. On a natural level, we can understand that God tends to say things that really put us over the top. Knowing who we are is very important. I must know who I am. No "If's," "And's" or "But's" about it.

In these times we get our Call confused. We think at times if sister so and so, or brother so and so, has a word of knowledge, automatically we assume that he or she is a prophet or prophetess. I will go further, lets say that he or she has the gift to start with, maybe God used that person in that gifting like he would use a donkey, doesn't mean the person has the Call of a prophet. It could be possible but we must never assume, because assumption is the cousin of accusation. It's dangerous sometimes to just presume events in our everyday lives, only then that spirit of assumption, and accusation will begin to cling on you. Falling into these pitfalls of the adversary will cause you to commence an assuming spirit, interpreting things by the optical lens of assumption, accusation, and gossip. Be attentive of that. This is how the devil plays with your mind. He tries to steal what was spoken to you, to kill the hope you have in your heart for the Call, and the Word given, to destroy your faith. You read once before how I use the "steal, kill, and destroy" method. The devil doesn't have that right, authority, and/or power, unless you give it to him. Praise God for Jesus! So when you ask God, "Lord who do you say, that I am?" When He answers with any of the five-fold ministry, accept it. Or, any other call for that matter, I tell you right now beloved to take it by force relentlessly!

*The kingdom of heaven suffers violence, and the violent take it by force.*
**Matt. 11:12** *(NKJV)*

God will not force you to do something you don't want to do. He will nudge your spirit. When He sees that you are not budging and always fighting His Spirit, this is when He will stop. This could be months or even years later. The day will come when He will no longer push you to do what He wills. Once you do say 'yes' to walk in your Call, do not look back when you begin to plow, or you will not be fit for the Kingdom of Heaven.

It takes awhile for the call on your life to actually take fruition. As time goes on you will recognize a difference in the natural because of the result of the spiritual, inviting you into a place called the wilderness period. Yes, we wait on the Lord; I believe its how you wait, that is very important. You must always be in an attitude of prayer and obedience. I have mentioned this several times for the reason that it is imperative to the hearts and minds of the believer. This whole chapter is dedicated to the life of someone who is wondering, "Who does God say that I am, in the body of believers, for the Glory of God?" Or, maybe confusion has settled in and you needed clarity.

*For God is not the author of confusion but of peace, as in all the churches of the saints.*
**1 Cor. 14:33** *(NKJV)*

God will remind you over and over again, that He will not leave you in the dust like some folks in the Church. If everything else fails, and no one else is there for you when you need him or her, don't fret; He is always there especially when you think He left to a distant land. Times of testing will visit you on diverse occasions. Scriptures are provided below to encourage and strengthen you, when you start feeling weary. Bear in mind, you can use these passages to help build up your faith, and strengthen you with your walk with Christ.

*Finally, my brethren, be strong in the Lord and in the power of His might.*
**Eph. 6:10** *(NKJV)*

*Not by might nor by power, but by My Spirit,' Says the* LORD *of hosts.*
**Zech. 4:6** *(NKJV)*

*Do not be afraid nor dismayed because of this great multitude, for the battle is not yours, but God's.*
**2 Chron. 20:15** *(NKJV)*

*The LORD shall fight for you, and ye shall hold your peace.*
**Ex. 14:14** *(KJV)*

*It is of the LORD'S mercies that we are not consumed, because his compassions fail not. They are new every morning: great is thy faithfulness. The LORD is my portion, saith my soul; therefore will I hope in him. The LORD is good unto them that wait for him, to the soul that seeketh him.*
**Lam. 3:22-25** *(KJV)*

## WHO AM I?

It took me awhile to accept who I am in the eyes of the Lord. He told me in 2002, that I was His apostle. I didn't even know what apostle's do, or even think they existed. Who am I to argue with God, and say He is wrong? Then confirming it down the road through a couple of evangelists, it was like they knew my life. I'd say this would be the seventh time God has said to me, specific timely prophetic words through people I did not know. We were invited one evening by a good friend of mine to visit a church for a five-day revival. Later on that night, my wife got excited to go worship God with other believers at this church down the road from our home. There was a dynamic anointed speaker by the name of Evangelist Donna, who was speaking that night. As the service was drawing to a close, she came straight toward us and said under the anointing, "Sir, Madam, you and your wife are called to be an Apostle and a Prophetess to the nations, since your mothers womb." On and on she went, it was like she knew us personally. The Holy Spirit was a lot more specific this time around. (In order to get to the new level we had to step on the old devil).

Providentially, about three weeks later we were invited to another meeting. This time it was to see Evangelist Ted Shuttlesworth who in turn was associated with the Late Mr. R.W. Shambach, a true weapon of God. My wife didn't understand why I was so excited. Little did my wife know I would watch Brother Shuttlesworth on his program "Faith Alive" on Trinity Broadcasting Network. The next morning, my wife and I woke up early Sunday morning to get ready for church. While she was in the bedroom, I entered into the bathroom and prayed to the Lord for guidance and clarity. I have been hearing so many voices around me of who I am and what I was not, kind of left me up in the air. Before I walked out of the bathroom, I asked the Holy Spirit to confirm this 'Big Call' we have on our lives, to go preach the gospel to the nations of the earth. Personally, that is a big call to handle. On June 28th 2009, during the service, we had a pastor giving us the order of service about Evangelist Shuttlesworth coming from out of town to speak that morning, and every night for the next six days. We were so excited and couldn't wait for service to begin. When service began the anointing of the service was very heavy. The anointing of God was so strong I didn't realize evangelist Ted was walking toward us. By our surprise, he calls us up to stand in front of about 1,200 witnesses. God confirmed and validated my wife and I in front of everyone who doubted us, and to those who did not believe we were righteous and holy in the sight of God. Brother Ted had this service set up to play again later on the Internet, and also his program on TBN, on Faith Alive. Under the power of the anointing Brother Ted, gave us a Word from the Lord, confirming every detail that was said to us, weeks and months before, by believers who walk in the five-fold ministry.

## 'O YE OF LITTLE FAITH

Prior to all of this, I had a reason not to believe and ended up in a state of confusion. Since lay members, pastors, and other ministers, started claiming apostles do not exist today, my faith was declining. Claiming that my wife and I are not real believers. The list can go on and on. My own family didn't believe me saying, "I don't know about this Luis, you really need to pray, go to church, and wait and see where in the ministry God needs you." "Go sit under a pastor and let him guide you." The Lord told me, that I am not to be under a pastor, pastors are to be under me. The church that I will build, setting up staff and then to ascertain church government in its proper format. It blew my mind as the fulfillment of God and His Word is becoming stronger and more evident as the days go by. Many didn't and still do not understand the call of an apostle for the fact no one is teaching who we are and what we can do in this age. Nevertheless, I have been waiting on God for over 10 years, when I first heard the call and hid! He has been calling me, and I kept dodging Him, so He did this in front of everyone so there won't be a reason for me to be in hiding. I tell you, God will find you wherever you go it makes no difference to Him. Praise God, for Jesus! As I was saying, all the counterfeits, mixed with the hypocrites started declaring that I don't know what I am talking about and that kind of call was not true. Saints, this is a prime example out of many, to think twice who you share your visions with. Furthermore, families sometimes could be worse than friends. Sadly, sometimes you will find more grace and mercy from the mouth of sinners than Christians! Some Christians will eat you alive!

*Where can I go from Your Spirit? Or where can I flee from Your presence? If I ascend into heaven, You are there; if I make my bed in hell, behold, You are there. If I take the wings of the morning, and dwell in the uttermost parts of the sea, even there Your hand shall lead me; And Your right hand shall hold me.*
**Psalms 139:7-10** *(NKJV)*

In my defense, when I was being attacked, I stated, "The Call was not from man, but from the Holy Spirit of God!" There wasn't much to say after that, some have held their peace. Beloved, I tell you the truth; you will still have those who will not believe the ministry the Lord has for you. Nevertheless, you go forth and do what God has commissioned you to do, in spite of what people say. You continue to believe God and press forward in all that you do for Him. Now I know, who I am in the Lord, and no one can take that away from me, but me. Like the saying goes, when God opens a door what man can ever close it!

*For I neither received it from man, nor was I taught it, but it came through the revelation of Jesus Christ.*
**Gal. 1:12** *(NKJV)*

## FIGHT FOR THE CALL

God had to remind me over and over again that He just simply loves me. He said this to me one day—it meant so much to me. "If you don't feel like anyone loves you, know that I love you." Those words resonated in my heart. Its like He knew what I was thinking before I even thought it. He is so awesome, especially when He speaks to me. Once I knew the Call and accepted it, Man! I tell you, its like all hell broke loose into my life.

## CALL? WHAT CALL?

I knew a pastor once, who was called to be an apostle through various prophets and evangelists who would visit the church confirming what was spoken to him before. In his disobedience he rejected *the call* for the reason he was going through to much distress and chaos as a pastor. He told me in his church one day, "Imagine if I accept the Call of apostle, man, more demons and more problems will come my way." What he failed to recognize and realize, the higher you are in the anointing of the Spirit, the more power you will have to endure to fight Satan's devils, warlocks, evil legions, witches, and every other realm of darkness is out their that opposes you. Don't let fear, doubt, and an unbelieving heart; which this was plainly the case, overtake you, or you will not prosper. It can stop the flow of the Holy Ghost to come in and move the way He really wants to in your life. A contorted spirit of bitterness and unforgiveness can settle, and clearly this has become the case toward me for sharing the Word, but the forgiveness I illustrated to him was much greater, even though he has rejected me. We must demonstrate love at a higher level and be the mature one who is willing to fall on the lap of the Ancient of Days, loving anyone under His power and anointing. All in all, as I walked and have gone into a path of my share of men denying who I really am, caused me to struggle all the more of accepting whom God called me to be, but in all my years I've never let it stop me from pressing toward the mark that is set before me, I will fulfill my destiny! And before I had this attitude of pressing in, hesitation still arose in my thinking.

Accepting the fact that God still loved me after all my mess-ups I pressed on. In addition, abandoned by people, after they put me through various kinds of hurt, pain, misery, and failure. There is one operative word that I just mentioned was such a big one for me, Ah, the word, "Failure." I felt like a failure as a son, a business owner, a man, a father, and a husband, never really accomplishing anything worth conversing about. It cut me down to the very core with no one to my left or my right to build me up, enlighten, or encourage me. You have to realize that God will never deal with you the way He deals with another. Learning the hard way and going forward on my own with The Almighty was all that I needed, but not everyone can be dealt the same cards that was handed down to me. The Holy Spirit, Christ Himself taught me and called me and not man similar to the apostle Paul: *"But I make known to you, brethren, that the gospel which was preached by me is not according to man. For I neither received it from man, nor was I taught it, but it came through the revelation of Jesus Christ"* (Galatians 1:12).

Assuredly, I would go to church service, and when I attended it really took a lot out of me when several times I would know things years ahead in advance. Further, some leaders, teachers, pastors and regular churchgoers would not always understand my calling and the revelations given to me by the Lord. We are different and unique individuals. There will be people that you are able to reach that a different person can't, and vise versa. Winning souls is the name of the game. God really loves you and adores you, male or female, Jew or gentile makes no difference to God. On a greater level, no matter in the least He can change you, whether you are a murderer, a thief, or a sex offender, if you are guilty of any of these, with the added hurt and pain having been ostracized, exploited, and gossiped about, God will accept you when you come to Him with a repented heart and a humble spirit. Society will treat you irrational and call you a monster, and indeed the very act and the destruction to the victim is evil, but God will turn it around and call you blessed, highly favored, and a new creation. He will heal you and the victim especially to those who come to Him in a state of penitence from their wicked ways. Once more, He will heal the victim to a higher degree you can ever imagine or conjure up in his or her own hearts and make them new. But, we must turn to Him and forgive others and ourselves for the act we did not invite, and those who caused it. He called several men and women in the Scriptures, that were worse off and He used them for His glory. The Lord always run after the unwanted, the unsuccessful, the beaten, the raped, the molested, the unattractive, the rejected, and mold them into fine gold of greater value then before. He uses the broken hearted, the hated, the forgotten, the non-educated, the lost, and the hungry as well as the rich, the educated, and successful. All things, all people, the Eyes of Compassion uses anyone in low and high positions in life. What I've experienced is God's way of breaking people. He loves to use broken people for His glory. Weakness in His sight is strong, the lowly, and the humble, will bear engaging fruit in the sight of others with no problem, prepared to walk in that strength. Did He not say pride comes before a fall? In order for you to know who you are you have to have Jesus' Spirit living on the inside of you. Knowing your true self and finding your position of purpose in the Lord will always give you the upper hand. People play games constantly with the grace that has been given freely, my question is, "Are we to carry on in foolishness and mock His holiness?" Scriptures say, God cannot be mocked, for what a man sows that shall he also reap, I would be very careful." You can amuse yourself with certain things, without becoming an obstacle to yourself and those around you, as long as you take serious the things of your Creator and keep it in its rightful place. This is the real deal jack! If you want to know who you are, you must give your life to Christ, and stay with Christ. Then, and only then, you can find your identity.

He is the only Truth that exists on the earth, there is no other (See John 14:6).

Always be in a mode to say **yes** to God when He needs you. You will not regret it. I hear people all the time say that we are not worthy. I know what they mean fundamentally, but on the other hand if we were not worth it, Jesus would have never come down to die for us, and God would not have sent Him in the first place, if we weren't worthy. He will never tell you to do something to hurt you or to destroy you, He loves you too much to lose His relationship with you after it took years for you to come and be saved the first time He called you. The only thing that can destroy you is if you blaspheme His Holy Spirit. I believe if we did it out of ignorance while we were in the world, it would be different. Simply, if you knew full well about the Lord and His Word and you blasphemed His Spirit, the high price you would have to pay will stagger you into throwing in the towel, knowing your life is finally over, even while you live. Dealing with sanctified people who fall in these various pits and trying to keep them in right standing with Jesus is complex on occasion. The reason for this is because ministry can be tough, and very strenuous to work for God and His people. I am sure you would agree with me if you are in ministry yourself that their will be moments it is easy but on occasion it could be onerous. You would understand at first why Moses acted out in anger, and stress, it was for the reason of tens of thousands coming to him with their complaints and grumbling. To put it in perspective, regarding the ministry and the Spirit of God, as you deal with the children of the Most High is the fact of making sure we do not walk in rebellion, and blaspheme the Spirit who is doing the work. If anyone blasphemes knowingly, then I say to that individual to live his or her life to the fullest, because you will not be forgiven in this world, or the world to come. You know what that is, to be never forgiven for all eternity? It's a life full of anger, hopelessness, and an utter disaster to the fullest extent, with a future of lost dreams and eternal anguish, bathing in fire!

*Wherefore I say unto you, all manner of sin and blasphemy shall be forgiven unto men: but* **the blasphemy against the Holy Ghost shall not be forgiven unto men**. *And whosoever speaketh a word against the Son of man, it shall be forgiven him: but whosoever speaketh against the Holy Ghost, it shall not be forgiven him, neither in this world, neither in the world to come.*
**Matt. 12:31-32** *(KJV)* Emphasis added.

Learning how to deter negative people and wicked spirits through people, you have to reach for Christ with all you've got. You do not have time for someone else to tell you who you are. Ask Christ the Lord with boldness and confidence, "Lord, who do you say that I am?" Expect an answer, I guarantee you, without a shadow of a doubt He will tell you. If His Divine Seed, which is the Holy Spirit, lessen in absence from the womb of your heart, then you will never make it to the wedding table in His Holy Heaven. Take dominion for what is right with the intention to put your mess into proper alignment, the Lord will bless you beyond measure for your efforts.

# CHAPTER FIVE

# THE CROSS AND THE CONQUEROR

# Chapter Five

=====================================

# THE CROSS AND
## THE CONQUEROR

*Yet in all these things we are more than
conquerors through Him who loved us.*

**—Romans 8:37**

*For the message of the cross is foolishness to
those who are perishing, but to us who are
being saved it is the power of God.*

**—1 Corinthians 1:18**

THE CROSS OF CHRIST IS A VERY powerful symbol, which
represents the nature of God's 'Big Idea' in how He used it
to defeat His enemies: Satan, death, and sin. The preaching
of the Cross is foolishness to those perishing because of the
natural man. While I'm on the subject of the Cross let me
share a symbol with you, which would look very familiar.

## THIS IS **NOT** A "PEACE" SIGN

Poignant as it seems. I have seen hundreds, if not thousands of born again Christians in this country and around the world with this symbol around their necks, belts, and their clothing; scores of others tattooed this pagan symbol on themselves without realizing what this actually means. It's true what Hosea the prophet said in the timely Scriptures, affirming that God's people are destroyed for a lack of knowledge, an absence of important information. This paganical symbol with the cross of Christ upside down with the arms broken downward literally means: *Christianity is defeated and the work done on the Cross is ailing!*

Going further, throughout the last 2,000 years this symbol has designated hatred of Christians. Nero, who loathed Christians, being part of the ten persecutions in the past had the apostle Peter crucified on a cross upside down. This repugnant event resembled the "Teutonic" (Germanic people or their language) cross and became a popular paganistic emblem of their day. Thereafter, this symbol became recognized as the "Neronic cross." The peace symbol is also called and known as the:

- ➤ Broken Cross
- ➤ The Crow's foot
- ➤ Christianity is defeated
- ➤ Witch's foot
- ➤ Nero Cross

- ➤ Sign of the "Broken Jew"
- ➤ Symbol of the "Anti-Christ"
- ➤ Gesture of despair
- ➤ The death of mankind

This is a satanic symbol Satanists would use to worship Satan with the "V" shape in the inside, which the founder of Satan's church, Anton Levey glorified. The "V sign" has a multihued history. "V" is the sign of the Romans for the number five. Dr. Adam Weishaupt who was the founder of the *Illuminati*, May 1st, 1776, He was the professor of Cannon Law at the University of Ingolstadt, Bavaria, Germany, used the symbol for his Illuminati to signify the "Law of Fives."

In the Kabbalah, the Hebrew letter "V" for "Van" is "Nail." Within the brotherhood of Satanism 'The Nail' is one of the secret titles of Satan. Why else does he use the Penta-gram through humans? (Penta means five) and the Five-fold salute is used in Masonry and witchcraft. This makes you think about throwing up the "peace sign" with your hands again. Having this information stored in the back of your mind will keep you in the safe zone with God and from the iniquitous campaigns of "the man of lawlessness." In the same course, as you strive and go full speed ahead with vigor in your commitments to the Lord, you will come to a place of understanding your motives and attitudes of how you think and speak with your own soul.

The soul contains your will, emotions, and your intellect. Making it a little simplified here are four kinds of men in the world. The Carnal man, the Natural man, the Spiritual man, and the Two-fold man.

**Carnal Man** (Flesh) - having the five senses which makes us world conscious for a four dimensional world. (Taste, touch/feeling, smell, hear, sight and time).

**Natural Man** (Soul) - makes us self-conscious, awareness-intelligence/soulish.

**Spiritual Man** (Spirit) - makes us God conscious, to perceive the divine things of God.

**Two-fold Man** (Flesh & Soul) - waivers on a constant basis, unstable in all his/her ways—sometimes devilish.

A **Carnal-minded** person doesn't believe Heaven or Hell, God or Devil exists. Believing with the philosophy–If I can see it or touch it, I believe it. Persuaded to accept many things because there are no absolutes (Psalms 14:1 & Psalms 53:1).

A **Natural-minded** person utters if there is a God or a devil it makes no difference. "You believe what you believe and I will believe what I want to believe." For his conscience has been seared as a hot iron. Thinks a man dying on a cross is foolishness (1 Cor. 1:18 & 1 Tim. 4:2).

A **Spiritual-minded** person believes everything pertaining to the Scriptures and has the ability to distinguish the divine from the counterfeit. The cross of Christ in his mind *is* the power of God. He knows he needs God in all circumstances for he has been crucified with Christ and he no longer lives (1 Cor. 1:18 & Gal. 2:20).

A **Double-minded or Two-fold** person vacillates one thing and then a "care of this life" arrives and doesn't deem the Lord ending up losing heart. In one moment they believe God to fix their situation, the next day they believe in themselves to fix the same situation. One day they have faith, the next minute they are doubtful, question bound, full of worry, and fear. An oscillated kind of lifestyle swinging freely through the pendulum of speech, fixated on everyone else's feeble mentality of faith ignoring their wavering minds.

*But let him ask in faith, with no doubting, for he who doubts is like a wave of the sea driven and tossed by the wind. For let not that man suppose that he will receive anything from the Lord; he is a double-minded man, unstable in all his ways.*
**James 1:6-8** *(NKJV)*

*Draw near to God and He will draw near to you. Cleanse your hands, you sinners; and purify your hearts, **you double-minded**.*
**James 4:8** *(NKJV)* Emphasis added

*Never worry about anything. But in every situation let God know what you need in prayers and requests while giving thanks. Then God's peace, which goes beyond anything we can imagine, will guard your thoughts and emotions through Christ Jesus.*
**Philippians 4:6-7** *(Gods Word)*

Since we are comprised as a triune body (body, soul, spirit) like the Lord, man is always in search of something higher than himself. God has programmed us to worship Him in spirit and in truth. Basically, we are speaking spirits who have a soul and live in a body. This is basic Christianity 101. I advise anyone who holds fast to the Lord to make sure we are in the category as the spiritual minded person.

When attending college, a few professors would teach that human beings do not have a soul. I also heard another professor say, that we don't have a spirit. In recent studies and scientific research, I have found something very interesting and relevant to humans having a soul. Remarkably, morticians and scientists put this to the test to see if the body does have a soul within. Sadly, this institution had a handful of people who were nearing their last breath; they would have them lay on a weight scale divan, until they passed. When they did pass, every single one of there bodies became six-pounds lighter. I thought that was interesting knowing that God associates man with the number six throughout the Scriptures. In addition, it was interesting to know that our soul weighs six pounds.

## YOUR PERSONALITY?

In my research I have found that there are sixteen major personalities, but I only mention four below: Phlegmatic, Choleric, Melancholy, and Sanguine. They all have their own character traits. Others can operate in a mixture of all of them.

- **Phlegmatic** – unemotional, indifferent, composed, slow-moving attitude.

- **Choleric** – expresses strong emotion, passionate, easily angered; short-tempered.

- **Melancholy** – gloomy, down and depressed, pessimistic at times toward everything

- **Sanguine** – cheerful, loud, confident, optimistic, excited full of energy

Which personality do you have?

It may not be any of them, but probably close. This is only associated with the soulish realm. We get caught up in the flesh so much we tend to forget the things we do and say, so as to protrude from the center of our soul. The excuse of, "That's just the way I am, that is my personality, I was born like this so if you love me, then you need to accept me for who I am." I have good news, you don't have to choose that kind of attitude; in turn it falls in line of a spirit of Jezebel, release, repent, rebuke, and be restored, for the devil is a liar! You don't have to become a label of your circumstance nor who your parents are or were, even your upbringing. There are no barriers with God. We must be transformed by the renewing of our minds. It's the soul that gets renewed not our spirit. Reach out your hand toward the heavens and let the "Father of lights" hold you once again, whether you are a backslider, saved, or a sinner. He loves you just where you are! We don't go to church because our lives are together. We go to church for the reason that our lives are jacked up with so many different everyday issues, with the aim of needing the Sitting Savior. He sits on the right-hand side of God. This means His work has been fully completed.

## NEVER GIVE UP ON YOUR RELATIONSHIP

Don't you desire to sit sometimes?

I am sure you do.

Men, you need rest from the weariness of the world's pressures and learn to spend time loving your wife and family, and find time to hold them all over again like you have done so many times before.

Woman, you need to reflect once again to refresh yourself with the "Human Well," the Lord Jesus, since your passions are not burning in you the way it used to.

Singles and the married will face challenges that can sometimes destroy what is really stirring in their hearts. I have met a decent amount of folks who were willing to pave their way into a frenzy desiring to give up on relationships that have gone sour. As I have been stating all along, mull over and consider yourself a conqueror! You serve a Big God! No problem you or the world system could create will ever be greater than your God. Giving up is not an option; embrace what was handed down to you encircled with the people you love. Encounter a new thing with Him and think twice about your marriage, I pray in the name of Almighty Jesus to come and rekindle the flame that once blazed in the ocean of your heart. Christian, I am familiar of the issue that surrounds your emotions and intelligence I've been there. I was married, but I didn't have a marriage, learning how to have one was a long process, and in the end it was worth it.

Jesus is the answer to convince, to display, and bring new wine into your old wine skins. He will never give up on you! Not ever! He did it for my wife and I, and we are no better than you. He restored us to His fullness in Him and He continues to do so 'til this day. He will do it for you as well, never a respecter of persons. He is the "volume" for your song, the "speaker" for your frequency, the "wind which carries His voice" into parabolic phrases of His Great Power! Formula: Learn to trust God and lean on His understanding, for His mercy endures forever. (See Proverbs 3:5, 6).

## FOLLOW THE LEADER

Now with this holy understanding of who Christ is, we still must worship God in spirit, which is our inner man born again, renewed by salvation according to Romans 10: 9,10 and John 4:24. In order for us to reach God and walk in the power and might of the Lord of Hosts, we mustn't shy away from correction or the conviction of the Holy Spirit within us. If you do ignore the prompting of the Spirit of God when you sin, you will slowly fall away. Jude vs 24, declares, "Now unto

Him is able to keep us from falling." We are not invincible. The views given by the New Testament writers were very clear it is possible for us to fall, but the Lord is there to get us back up, if we heed to His voice. Following the leading of the Holy Spirit is a necessity in our lives to be able to follow Christ daily. He is the one that would allow the cross to enter into our minds and penetrate our hearts.

The time has come to fall into the hands of the cross. The Almighty Christ has all the supremacy and authority to save the souls of hurting men, woman, the young, the old, and the lost all around the world. Beloved, I rather be a fool speaking one line of truth, then to speak ten thousand words of pure emptiness. Souls are my main objective. I am writing and speaking to make sure we all have the opportunity to make a decision to accept Christ, especially to those that are not saved. Essentially, I teach and preach to the saved to keep them saved and to the lost to lead them to salvation. Our passion should convert into a tireless compassion, enabling us to target everyone and anyone who walks with the "Breath of lives" in their body, being a perfect Image Bearer of God, who needs the opportunity to be saved. No color, no race, no creed, or religion should ever stop us at all! I tried, Jehovah Witness Kingdom Hall, Catholicism, Islam, and Secular Humanism, you name it. None of these religions or their ministers was there for me when I was going through so much hell in my life and needed a way of escape of my complexity. Jesus our Messiah, the world's "Paragraph," the world's "Essay," and the world's "Word Walker," must be heard and boasted about to all flesh–laying the flesh and our souls down in submission– now!

Mass quantities of believers are allowing too much foolishness, sinful desires, scandal, and many other sins I am too ashamed to even write about. Back in the ancient days of Jerusalem, God would not allow such drama and mayhem to take place in His Temple, you would have to walk blameless and holy in His sight at all times. We must unite hand in hand and love each other unconditionally. There is not enough love going around in our churches today. In the days of the apostles, we had one say, "I am from John," "Well I am from Barnabas," "oh yeah, and I am from Apollos." This is pure imprudence in the eyes of God seeing we still do this to this day. "Well I am from Assemblies of God we believe in baptizing in the Father, Son and Holy Ghost," "Well I am from Church of God in Christ we believe in this" Well I am Southern Baptists we don't speak in that." And the list goes on and on. The devil couldn't beat the church; why not make numerous denominations to cause conflict and division within the church body? Guess what? He actually progressed in that area, knowing we are at each other's throats right in front of the Masters face blasting each other with our doctrine. Pastors are not getting along with other pastors, because of various arguments, and the big one is, worrying about pastor so and so stealing members. Lets get this straight; no one can steal any one from any one. No more than a man stealing another man's wife. People leave on their own, simply because they wanted to leave, not for the reason of being "stolen." Foolishness such as this is not getting the Body of Christ in order. We have to be ready for the coming of God's Christ! All that He is, and what He killed on the cross was all of our sins and iniquity, we must not hold any record of wrongdoings amongst our brothers and sisters in Christ. Do not compare yourself to others, and become jealous, or allow a spirit of envy to creep and slip into the door of your heart, let it knock, but do not open.

*For we dare not class ourselves or compare ourselves with those who commend themselves. But they, measuring themselves by themselves, and comparing themselves among themselves, are not wise.*
***2 Cor. 10:12*** *(NKJV)*

*Guard your heart more than anything else…*
***Prov. 4:23*** *(Gods Word)*

The cross is the amazement of God's miraculous love, and true caring of His creation. In times before we were a people without hope and no God in the world, our world of sin collided with the world of purity, and never came to a suitable union, until Jesus died bringing it all together into one. We as a people, a body, must come into agreement with the Lord, and make sure His will is done in and for our lives as well as others.

## MORE THAN CONQUERORS

The Conqueror, are those who are born from above with His Spirit breathing and living within your inner man.

*Yet in all these things we are more than conquerors through Him who loved us.*
**Romans 8:37** *(NKJV)*

The Bible says that we are **more** than conquerors, not just conquerors. We need to thank God for this privilege, and the apostle Paul confers his persuasion regarding God's love. Unfortunately, in these last days, we have a big problem demonstrating love to our fellow believer and to our enemies. Where is the love of Christ? Yes–it seems difficult at times but when you have a relationship with your Master, He helps us with His Spirit if we yield.

*And walk in love, as Christ also has loved us and given Himself for an offering, a sacrifice and us to God for a sweet-smelling aroma.*
**Eph. 5:2** *(NKJV)*

*Which has come to you, as it has also in the entire world, and is bringing forth fruit, as it is also among you since the day you heard and knew the grace of God in truth...*
**Col. 1:6** *(NKJV)*

*But I say to you, love your enemies, bless those who curse you, do good to those who hate you, and pray for those who spitefully use you and persecute you, that you may be sons of your Father in heaven; for He makes His sun rise on the evil and on the good, and sends rain on the just and on the unjust...*
**Matt. 5:44-45** *(NKJV)*

We must illustrate love, be holy and pure in His sight and in the sight of men. One way of putting that into practice is by driving back from our wants and preventing ourselves to be placed in a position that would cause us to fall into sin, this is the duty of every believer. Everyone, at some point repents from the sin they committed but we are not to stay there. We have to think, speak and **be** conquerors! Do not **act** like a conqueror it will only be just that–acting. If a person keeps toddling in this disposition he will only become an actor or a performer instead of a man or woman of God who is truly walking in total holiness and compliance. The Bible states, "If God be for us who can be against us."

*If God is for us, who can be against us?*
**Romans 8:31** *(NKJV)*

*For as many as are led by the Spirit of God, these are sons of God.*
**Romans 8:14** *(NKJV)*

You are not obscure, indistinct, dark, faint, or remote. All things in human life relate to God someway, shape, or form. Us as the Body of Christ, and you as an individual, are His alone. You are important. He needs His warriors out there leading unbelievers to Christ. Setting a path to uprightness, sanctity, and tranquility. You cannot give up on yourself or other people so easily. Compassion and love is the essence of the heart of God. To hold and hug those who find it unfamiliar, with the willingness of being able to receive such fervor. The Word of God does not come back to Him void, but will accomplish all that God has spoken. It's the same thing when we prophesy into someone's life. We are not to say anything to someone that will discourage knowing we reap what we sow. We must make things right, right now. It is unfortunate to have members backbiting and relying on false words and creative thoughts to ramble in the minds of the Christian. If you have something against your brother, you must leave your gift at the altar. So when you reconcile with your brother or sister, you will be able to have a clean heart in the eyes of God to represent your gift. Building each other up is God's will. Never think we are in the business to tear down and demolish one another. As a believer, we are never too lax our own. Our job is to bring comfort and encouragement. Here are the four E's, which are the duties of every Image Bearer:

**Exhortation** – to urge, and advise strongly.

**Edification** – to improve the moral character or mind of a person.

**Encouragement** – to inspire with confidence and hope.

**Empathy** – the capacity for participating in an understanding the feelings or ideas of another.

## THE BACKSLIDERS

God is married to the backslider, as Jeremiah the prophet so eloquently put it. As you keep reading if the individual doesn't repent, they will not make it into heaven. As harsh as it sounds, it is the Word of the Lord. As a watchman, who is a prophet, I must warn God's people. Standing for truth and endurance in the Spirit is the heart of a watchman.

*When I say to the wicked, 'You shall surely die,' and you give him no warning, nor speak to warn the wicked from his wicked way, to save his life, that same wicked man shall die in his iniquity; but his blood I will require at your hand. Yet, if you warn the wicked, and he does not turn from his wickedness, nor from his wicked way, he shall die in his iniquity; but you have delivered your soul. Again, when a righteous man turns from his righteousness and commits iniquity, and I lay a stumbling block before him, he shall die; because you did not give him warning, he shall die in his sin, and his righteousness, which he has done, shall not be remembered; but his blood I will require at your hand. Nevertheless if you warn the righteous man that the righteous should not sin, and he does not sin, he shall surely live because he took warning; also you will have delivered your soul.*
**Ezek. 3:18-21** *(NKJV)*

*If the watchman sees the sword coming and does not blow the trumpet, and the people are not warned, and the sword comes and takes any person from among them, he is taken away in his iniquity; but his blood I will require at the watchman's hand...*

*When I say to the wicked, 'O wicked man, you shall surely die!' and you do not speak to warn the wicked from his way, that wicked man shall die in his iniquity; but his blood I will require at your hand. Nevertheless if you warn the wicked to turn from his way, and he does not turn from his way, he shall die in his iniquity; but you have delivered your soul.*
**Ezek. 33:6,8,9** *(NKJV)*

Saints, I recommend you to do extraordinary things for the Lord you have never done before. Visit the sick and pray with them to be healed. Give, and it will be given back to you. Whether in loving kindness, money, even borrowing your life for their time, your Maker can take you to a higher level if done with the right motive when you help others. You are a channel, and as a channel of God you are to assist those in need, which in turn brings exaltation.

*Give, and it will be given to you: good measure, pressed down, shaken together, and running over will be put into your bosom. For with the same measure that you use, it will be measured back to you.*
**Luke 6:38** *(NKJV)*


## SEIZE YOUR LEGACY

Seizing the proper significance of being a conquering Christian, who intermingles their character close to the cross, will lay a foundation of a legacy beyond the four corners of the globe. Paul did the exact same thing and sent the message all across the known planet, having an impact of hope, with anticipation in his soul to see the Lord again. Jesus came to give life and to give it to the fullest without us ever being able to lose it. Your life will be redefined in the highest quarter when those around you think of you. A legacy of a winning attitude, and a contrite spirit containing the essence of tranquility and poise, elevating you to another level in Christ Jesus for the glory of God the Father.

*I have been crucified with Christ; it is no longer I who live, but Christ lives in me; and the life, which I now live in the flesh I live by faith in the Son of God, who loved me and gave Himself for me.*
**Gal. 2:20** *(NKJV)*

# CHAPTER SIX

# IN SPIRIT AND IN TRUTH

# Chapter Six

---

# IN SPIRIT AND
# IN TRUTH

*But the hour is coming, and now is, when the true
worshipers will worship the Father in spirit and truth,
for the Father is seeking such to worship Him.*

**—John 4:23**

WHEN YOU PRAY IN THE SPIRIT, in your heavenly language,
demons do not understand because you are speaking mysteries
to God. Psalms 150:6 states "Let everything that has breath,
Praise the Lord." How can people praise the Lord, exactly?
Well, they can praise the Lord in their own language by
using God's universal tongue. I know many believers do not
think nor believe that tongues are for today, but they speak
in a tongue, nevertheless. Some Bible scholars and other
denominations might not believe in speaking in tongues,
declaring it was only for the early church. What do I mean?
If you think about it, HALLELU-YAH is a universal heavenly
language given by God to prove that He exists! For example:
How do we, "Praise the Lord" in God's universal tongue,
which is, "Halleluyah," in your own language? Answer? It's
Halleluyah.

In *Chinese:* Halleluyah! In *English*: Halleluyah! In *Afrikaans*:
Halleluyah! In *German*: Halleluyah! In *Thai*: Halleluyah! In

*French*: Halleluyah. You get the picture? When we say Jesus, in any of these languages it sounds different. This alone to me proves that God exists. The Lord outsmarted the most intelligent being, with his intelligible explanations, knowing that man is very limited in his intelligence.

## WHAT'S HIS NAME?

For those who are not familiar with the 'tetragrammaton', of the Y-H-W-H a rendition of 'Yahweh' I will lay a small foundation in the 'four meaning'. Basically, the 'Jah' in Hallelu**jah** it is not pronounced with the 'Jah' but the 'Yah' sound. In the New King James version you will see the correct rendering in Psalms 68:4, Isaiah 12:2, Isaiah 26:4, and Isaiah 38:11, from 'Jah' to 'Yah' revealed four times in all of the Bible in accordance to the dead sea scrolls. It denotes the 'A' for Adonai and the 'E' denotes for Elohim, because the letter 'J' was invented approximately five hundred years ago, the letter 'J' or 'J' sound, in the Hebrew language did not exist, as well as vowels. Hence, Zionist's would pronounce Jesus, Yahshua or Yeshua meaning "Salvation Saves," 'Yah' is 'Salvation', and 'Shua', is 'Saves'. Yahshua or Yeshua also a derivative to the name 'Joshua'. Proving Jesus came in His Father's name.

*I have come in My Father's name, and you do not receive Me; if another comes in his own name, him you will receive.*
**John 5:43** *(NKJV)*

## REALITIES OF THE HEART

He is worthy to be praised, no matter what country, culture, barrier, or background you can think of in view of the fact that God, will break the back of demons and breakdown any wall that tries to counter Him. He will make sure that every praise, prayer, cry, and a spirit who worships, reaches His ear when it is coming from a heart that is untainted and pious. He is not impressed with eloquent speech and how sophisticated you can put words together, but how real your heart of compassion is toward Him. God is searching for a pure heart that has a desire to serve with no pessimistic motives involved. When you have compassion to serve, you are laying down the very fundamental nature of who you are. Moreover, you hit a point of wanting to surrender yourself no matter the cost, for who you are in Christ. The consecrated spirit in you has to connect with who God is. Intricately, your spirit has to be knit together with the will of the Father.

## THE WATCHMAN (Ezekiel 3 & 33)

Always stay faithful to your church no matter what, unless, they are teaching contrary to the Word of God. I encourage you to be a person of integrity and remain true to God and your leaders. The Bible says, "Obey those who have rule over you." Continue to be the peacemaker when all else is crumbling and falling apart. In all that you do in work or deed contend with a mind frame of complaining or murmuring (See Phil. 2:14). Do not encourage it by listening to the mess that comes out of the mouth of the person or persons. Walk in the Spirit and in the truth (John 14:6). Travel with someone that you can trust, on the basis you cannot inform everyone of all your personal secrets, issues, desires, visions, and plans, there are people who are not able to handle it, it will do more damage than good, occasionally. Other times, if you are not careful and you end up confessing private information about yourself to someone you felt you could be open with, and in the end you have become an icon of a bad situation of ridicule and gossip. This is a perfect example of discerning your associates and those you call your friends. Everyone in your circle of influence are not always compassionate about your personal matters, it will only bring contention and distress into your life that was unnecessary from the start.

Be in constant prayer and surround yourself with anointed people of God who can facilitate in the time of need, and encourage you whenever you need aid. You need that life support to help you breathe when the enemy is seeking to strangle your dreams, and aim to choke your visions right out of your heart and spirit. Don't just rebuke when the enemy comes against you like a flood, but expel, destroy, repel, and resist him in the name of Jesus, and God will raise that standard for you and with you. He will stand triumphantly, and so will you in the name of the Lord! Watch and pray always. As I said earlier, I know a "watchman" is considered a prophet in the Old Testament, but in other cases such as these, it's to watch out for yourself and others in the spirit. Be wise as a serpent and yet gentle as a dove. Fight back in the spirit and take back what the enemy has stolen from you, he has done enough after all these years of stealing, beating you down, and taking what never belonged to him in the first place.

I had to fight hard and get back what I allowed the devil to take from me. Now I know that Satan steals your visions, the devil destroys your spirit, and they both devour your dreams even though they are one in the same. This will only happen if you are unaware of the enemy's devices, tactics, and deceptions. You must understand that the enemy is very real, conniving and he plays for keeps, with the goal of making sure your future is dark, cold, and unbearable. There are Christians who state that Jesus is their love but are wolves in sheep's clothing. Moreover, Jesus talked about hell just as much as he did about heaven, since He knew that His Image Bearers would not imagine the fact, a loving God can create such a horrific place of torment for anyone, but reserved for Satan and his angels only. Essentially, I know for verity that hell exists, not only for the reason of the holy men of God who wrote the Bible, but for the actuality of being allowed to come out of my body, experiencing the spirit realm first hand. With that being said, I would like to assure you hell is a real and tangible place in the center of the earth, as recorded in the Scriptures. Let me refresh your memory, Jonah went to hell, Jesus went to hell, the rich man (Mr. Divies) went to hell. All the Old Testament prophets were in the center of the earth where hell was with only a chasm fixed between them. All people from ancient times before Christ died, went to paradise adjacent exactly where hell is located. When Jesus died on the cross, He relocated paradise from the heart of the earth, to reposition it into the third heaven, with a triumphal procession in the presence of His Father.

*For as Jonas was three days and three nights in the* **whale's belly***; so shall the Son of man be three days and three nights* **in the heart of the earth***.*
**Matt 12:40** *(KJV)* Emphasis added.

*Then I said, I am cast out of thy sight; yet I will look again toward thy holy temple. The waters compassed me about, even to the soul: the depth closed me round about; the weeds were wrapped about my head.* **I went down to the bottoms of the mountains***; the earth with* **her bars** *was about me forever: yet hast thou brought up* **my life from corruption***, O LORD my God. When my soul fainted within me,* **I remembered the Lord; and my prayer went up to You, into Your holy temple***.*
**Jonah 2:4-7** *(KJV)* Emphasis added.

*Then Jonah prayed unto the LORD his God out of the fish's belly, and said, I cried by reason of mine affliction unto the LORD, and he heard me;* **out of the belly of hell cried I***, and thou heardest my voice.*
**Jonah 2:1-2** *(KJV)* Emphasis added.

*Wherefore he saith, when he ascended up on high,* **he led captivity captive,** *and gave gifts unto men. Now that he ascended, what is it but that* **he also descended first into the lower parts of the earth**? *He that descended is the same also that ascended up far above all heavens, that he might fill all things.*
**Eph. 4:8-10** *(KJV)* Emphasis added.


You will not find mountains or an earth with bars inside of a whale's stomach; he died in the belly of the whale, which was symbolic, a parallel between Jesus and Jonah contrasting Jesus' death with Jonah. Jonah's soul started to descend and as he descended that's when he saw mountains, and then the bars of hell appeared in front of him. Jonah prayed and repented to God and the Lord heard his plea, causing the whale to vomit him out onto dry land. For all intents and purposes, friends, I caution you, it is an actual place with fire, fear, and undying hopelessness with no anticipation of ever getting out. Unfortunately, repentance does not exist after you already died in your sin and it becomes your eternal home. Its while you are yet alive, you make the decision now, to accept Christ so you do not get sent there forever, choosing a path either to die twice or live twice. If you consider physical death then it's really dying three times if you are in sin. Yes, according to Hebrews and Revelation, a sinner will die a natural death once and spiritually twice. The born again believer, will live twice, unless they experience natural death on earth. Let me explain: A sinner will die a natural death once on earth and then die a second time when placed in Hades, remember Jesus said that he is going to take Hades and cast it, into the Lake of fire which is considered Hell, that is the third time. When the New Testament was written in the Greek, the English translators replaced 'Hades' with 'Hell,' when in true essence 'Gehenna' is considered 'Hell', in the Gospels (Matt. 10:28 & Rev. 20:14). Revelation 14 is only speaking spiritual death, therefore, considering a "Second Death," Which path will you choose?

## Sinners/Backsliders Path

**Path 1**. A sinner dies physically, **once** > Sinner dies a **second** time spiritually and sent to hades/hell > Sinner dies a **third** time after the Great White Throne Judgment, which is a more horrible death then the second time, because the sinner is sent into the Lake of fire to be in the same place as the devil and his angels, the third time.

## Path of the Child of God

**Path 1**. A saint lives physically, **once** (if raptured) > Saint lives again for all eternity = **twice** lived

**Path 2**. A saint dies physically, **once** (not raptured) > Saint lives again for all eternity = died once and lives again

Hades or hell (which ever you feel most comfortable using) is considered to be like sweating in a very, very hot sauna. When the 'sinner' is placed into the lake of fire, with the devil and his angels, that same sinner will be in the exact location suffering torment in eternal agony and torture, for all eternity, because of his rejection of Christ as Lord and Savior. Word of warning: this is one of the main reasons Satan and his demons are trying very hard to get you back into sin and your old ways. His goal is to keep you where you are, making sure you don't get right with God, thus, your eternal future could be the same as his. Regrettably, there are thousands of Christians who do not believe there is a devil, or a literal hell. I believe if there was no hell than Jesus would have never revealed it through His prophets of old or to His ministers of today.

*If your hand causes you to sin, cut it off. It is better for you to enter into life maimed, rather than having two hands, to go to hell, into the fire that shall never be quenched. Where 'Their worm does not die, and the fire is not quenched.' And if your foot causes you to sin, cut it off. It is better for you to enter life lame, rather than having two feet, to be cast into hell, into the fire that shall never be quenched. Where 'Their worm does not die, and the fire is not quenched.' And if your eye causes you to sin, pluck it out. It is better for you to enter the kingdom of God with one eye, rather than having two eyes, to be cast into hell fire. Where 'Their worm does not die, and the fire is not quenched.'*
**Mark 9:43-48** *(NKJV)*

*…The soul that sinneth, it shall die.*
**Ezek. 18:4, 20** *(ASV & KJV)*

*And as it is appointed for men to die once, but after this the judgment.*
**Heb. 9:27** *(NKJV)*

*Is there not an appointed time to man upon earth? Are not his days also like the days of an hireling?*
**Job 7:1** *(KJV)*

*And do not fear those who kill the body but cannot kill the soul. But rather fear Him (God) who is able to destroy both soul and body in hell.*
**Matt. 10:28** *(NKJV)* Emphasis added.

God's eyes run to and fro looking for willing people to utilize for His ministry to be able to develop and strengthen the body of His Son.

*For the eyes of the LORD run to and fro throughout the whole earth, to show himself strong in the behalf of them whose heart is perfect toward him"*
**2 Chron. 16: 9** *(KJV)*

*For My eyes* are *on all their ways; they are not hidden from My face, nor is their iniquity hidden from My eyes.*
**Jer. 16:17** *(NKJV)*

*And there is no creature hidden from His sight, but all things* are *naked and open to the eyes of Him to whom we must give account.*
**Heb. 4:13** *(NKJV)*

And the devil always attempts to copy, mimic, and imitate the Lord since the very beginning of his fall (Isaiah 14 & Ezekiel 28). In an instant, Satan learned the hard way that he simply couldn't be greater than God. He is very well educated in the Scriptures better than most Christians, and impersonates the attributes of God as he becomes an angel of light throughout the course of history toward men, but in actuality he is a hurricane of horrendous destruction and despair. Everything that Satan touches spoils, plunders, and rots in his hands. He has no original ideas; his motto is "Why not become the great copycat, since I cannot be the Most High God?" In the Holy Verses you would realize what this kind of distorted thinking has done to him and the angels that followed after, resulting an everlasting stay in a world of eternal condemnation! 1 Peter 5:8 states, he goes to and fro in the regions of the earth seeking whom he may devour "Like" a roaring lion. "Like" in the text is considered a *simile*, a figure of speech, and an allegory. Therefore, he is **not** an actual lion, but he *acts* like one. He is an actor, and actor's act, but it's not the real story. How many agree that he is a lion with no teeth, with a ramshackled mane? Saints, he is a defeated foe, when Christ reigned champion over him at the cross—The Lion of the Tribe of Judah, triumphs over the one who is *like* a lion. Hallelujah!

*Be sober; be vigilant; because your adversary the devil walks about like a roaring lion, seeking whom he may devour. Resist him, steadfast in the faith, knowing that the same sufferings are experienced by your brotherhood in the world.*
**1 Peter 5:8-9** *(NKJV)*


## KINGDOM MINDED

Do not trust and rely on yourself for a supernatural exchange when you are walking after the flesh, you will walk into a well of trouble you don't want to encounter. Let the Holy Spirit breathe on you. Make love to the Lord in your time of Holy Communion in prayer. This is the key element to knowing Him. The "Almighty Him," loves you more than you can ever love yourself! He loves your children more than you will ever love them in a million lifetimes. We must learn to walk as conquerors; a conqueror knows when he or she is conquered by love. A conqueror is kingdom minded. There is a difference when compared to a regular Churchgoer. It's a vast difference comparing a child of God, to a Son of God. I mentioned earlier, a "Son" is a mature term, which means they are walking in their inheritance now. A child of God has to wait until they are mature enough to be able to handle and walk in their inheritance. One, who is a conqueror in the spirit, conquers in all areas of their life; this also is a character trait of a "Son." Not walking in defeat and vain words or lifestyles, but in obedience and prayer admonishing their pace carefully with discernment. Various folks will come to you seemingly harmless, but inside they are filled with conceit and dead men's bones.

The Lord desires for us to spend more time with Him. We must prepare for the coming of the Messiah. Part of the preparation is making sure our lives as a whole, is in total submission to the will of God. Jesus said, "Not my will, but yours be done." Kingdom mindedness always strives to rise above juncture and crisis. By no means I speak or write about issues I have not experienced myself. It's hypocritical for someone to instruct another without the conviction of making sure; he or she is doing the same thing that they teach to others. Be Kingdom minded, think big, follow the vision that is set before you, then take it and run with it, without looking back. Move forward and bring destruction to the chasms of hell, with every opportunity that comes your way. Win souls for the Glory of God the Father. In the name of Jesus! Go and advance the King's dominion by force!

*Yet in all these things we are more than conquerors through Him who loved us. For I am persuaded that neither death nor life, nor angels nor principalities nor powers, nor things present nor things to come, nor height nor depth, nor any other created thing, shall be able to separate us from the love of God, which is in Christ Jesus our Lord.*
**Romans 8:37-39** *(NKJV)*

A *True Kingdom* frame of mind is to love God with all their existence; the reason for that is, it helps you find your true character and uniqueness. In fact, He requires of us to love Him. He knows the devil is doing all he can to pull you away from eternal life. Do not go down without a fight, the enemy has lost the battle and the war. If you are not saved and you are in sin, labeled a child of disobedience, I implore you to think twice about the position you are in. After a while the enemy will come to you and try to take over your mind, heart, and eventually your spirit. Not having the Spirit of the Lord living in you will open a gateway for the devil to come in and sup with you, just like Jesus mentioned in the Book of Revelation. Remember Satan is the great counterfeiter, the great impersonator. He causes many souls that are already lost to **hate** God and His people to prevent them from entering into the joys of oneness, and partaking of Christ's kingdom. The devil hates the children's *Bread*; Jesus is the '*Bread*,' which has come down from heaven, keeping this in mind will make you wise to the devils methods.

There is a warning in the Word, which speaks about hating the Lord and not coming to grips of accepting who Jesus really is.

*But he who sins against Me wrongs his own soul; all those who hate me love death.*
**Prov. 8:36** *(NKJV)*

*He who believes in Him is not condemned; but he who does not believe is condemned already, because he has not believed in the name of the only begotten Son of God.*
**John 3:18** *(NKJV)*

## TRUTH REIGNS

Clearly, we know that preaching is proclamation and teaching is explanation. We need to teach more in our churches today. It's not enough to just preach what's already written, we need to go deeper with the Word of God. When someone is being challenged with something devastating they will need to be taught how to handle it because being inspired and motivated will not handle the situation. They are going to need proper teaching and instruction to overcome their circumstances. I am not saying preaching doesn't have its proper place, but sometimes we need to get the right teaching to receive the right results. Dividing the Word of truth and executing them into the bride of Christ lovingly and effectively. The apostle Paul was a teaching apostle. Writing mostly to the gentiles about the Messiah in his day. He had such a heavy concern and a burden toward his people, you could hear it in his voice entreating them, to walk on the road of salvation and redemption. In fact, Romans chapter six to nine is designated for the Jews. The Lord wanted him to address the gentiles only after the Jews kept rejecting his message about the death of Christ on the cross. After all, the Jews kept trying to take his life and forcing him into dreadful situations, to stop him from preaching the Light of life to all men.

Much can be learned from the apostles and the early church fathers, which worshipped God and trusted the Word completely and totally. That is the same attitude we must have as Christians *in the faith* today. Belief always has a beginning, *faith* always is. **F**ully **A**ware **I**n **T**rusting **H**im.

Evidently, the Lord's will is to make certain that His everlasting Words of freedom become obvious in the life of the believer. Not so with certain claims of heresy that I've encountered in the last several years, causing bondage to run throughout the nation of America and abroad. I have witnessed and experienced many ministers within the Body of Christ, taking passages out of context, making it a pretext just to fit their distorted views. Ministers in churches are teaching young people the Holy Scriptures, and after church preaching to others that they don't see anything wrong with fornication, because its not stated specifically in the Holy Bible. I believe in my heart and I am sure you agree, that fornication is a sin, is it not? If you are not married, then you shouldn't have sex with someone who is not your wife or husband. Consequently, the morality of churchgoers and leaders reverberated critical views that can really put a new believer into confusion. Especially, if they have a specific call on their life, such as, the office of apostle or bishop. Once, I had a pastor tell me that bishops are above apostles. What he failed to understand, is the *apostle* put those offices in place. They did not exist until the 'Great Apostle,' Jesus, came onto the scene to create others like Himself and set those offices in proper placement. Not all are called to be apostles, prophets, or pastors, but we must really teach in detail what each office of the five-fold ministry actually does. These issues are minuscule, compared to the real troubles that exist in the four walls of the church. At the same time, we have to be mindful of the little foxes that destroy the vine. Saints, understand, in the eyes of the Lord He doesn't base His prominence or thesis on how many degrees you have, or how systematic is your theology. He is concerned more about the way you live your life in complete obedience to Him and His Word. Like I have been saying, the Bible has such little depth a newborn believer can sip from it, but yet deep enough to drown the most celebrated theologian with all of his degrees. Don't get me wrong; I think Theological Seminary is wonderful. If, that is where God is calling you to, praise the Lord, you go for it in the name of Jesus. As long as the professor or yourself do not try to minimize the character, mannerisms, and how God manifests to His children, as others in some cases are doing.

The autonomy of God has complete capability to set up and break down kingdoms when He chooses to, with no permission from us. Putting God in a box like He is an action figure that they can pull out of their back pockets whenever they need to justify their sins is hazardous to your health— literally. It will only bring chaos and a fountain of perplexity. Focus, and good comprehension of spiritual themes will help you in the long run, to maintain your composure of certainty in the Son of Man, when the world throws you a curve ball of qualm.

Such beliefs really grab a hold of me, when I see major subjects being taken so lightly, especially in the community and on television. Galatians 5:16-21 specifically declares a listing of all kinds of transgressions that will prevent anyone who travels down the path of self-pleasure and loose living. One day my wife and I were watching a television program, and we came across a channel with someone advocating gay marriage and immoral behavior. I never say committing adultery is wrong. I never say that homosexuality is wrong. I say it's a sin! When you confess these immoral acts are wrong, the world knows how to go around the Word and make it right, and legalize it, as if they had the power to do so. In the end, the Lord will win and sin will have its day. Sin is sin, regardless how a person tries to deal with it or cover it up. When a man or woman cover their sins, they will not prosper in this life until they 1st repent, 2nd confess to God, 3rd ask for forgiveness, and forsakes it, this is when mercy will soon follow after.

*He who covers his sins will not prosper, but whoever confesses and forsakes them will have mercy.*
**Prov. 28:13** *(NKJV)*


## YOU MUST GET UNDERSTANDING

The multitudes of those who choose not to walk in total freedom, but desires to walk in the periphery of holiness will never fulfill the mission God has for their life, and will never come to the richness of the indwelling of the Holy Spirit. The navigation and imprint of God's hand have already been impressed with the truth, but if the Image Bearer doesn't get it straight, and begins to refuse the call that is on his or her life, he or she will be in a position of eternal discontentment. The Word declares plainly the person or persons are worthy of death! Your flesh must die, and be in a state of total surrender to God when you are walking in His presence. There are consequences, if humility and walking in truth with His Spirit, doesn't bring submission and total yielding in your reality. We will not be used of God if we become bound with a tradition that becomes greater than the Word of God. The Writers of the Bible, made it very clear when it declares; for all believers to cry out to God as 'Abba' to seek out His understanding, so when the command is given it will fall on a listening ear and an obedient soul. If we admonish our leaders who are guiding us into the arms of Christ we will fall flat on our faces. Spiritually, individuals will destroy themselves very quickly. In all things considering, deem the fact if the Christian will begin to wander away from the understanding that the Lord has set before him, he will receive warning after warning, with caution signs in every area in the natural from the spirit realm to repent and change your mind back to Him. The believer has to take into account that they will have to turn away from their disobedience immediately. Father God has mapped out the way clearly in His Son, all he or she has to do is walk into it and stay there with consistency and courage, without wavering.

...**Without understanding**, *covenant breakers, without natural affection, implacable, unmerciful: Who knowing the judgment of God, that* **they which commit such things are worthy of death**, *not only do the same, but have pleasure in them that do them.*
**Romans 1:31-32** *(KJV)* Emphasis added.

*The man that* **wandereth out of the way of understanding** *shall remain in the congregation of the dead.*
**Prov. 21:16** *(KJV)* Emphasis added.

## NO LIMITATIONS

What happens in a Christian's life who really serves the Lord? The Spirit of God starts teaching you things that others will not understand. Dreams unexplainable and yet so vivid with a hidden message will make you curl where you stand. The message is clear, direct and you get excited and cannot wait to see what else God has already planned for you, with anticipation. Then visions begin to occur when you are awake, demonstrating futuristic events to get you to start moving forward in the Lord. These visions are sometimes so effervescent it feels like you can grab it and taste it. The moment you share it with others just like Joseph did with his brothers, people will end up hating you or become jealous, even distant. There are the select few that will help you celebrate and assist with shared enthusiasm, and that's what I call spiritual motivators. As a man or woman of God you must be cautious in every area of your life, be meticulous with spiritual parasites, when they begin to raise their ugly head and try to drain you instantly. Furthermore, no matter where you are in the world, you will have the spiritual abilities of discerning who are spiritual parasites, and also spiritual hitch-hikers that want to take and pull from the gifting's that God has placed deep down inside of you. You have no indication, or a shadow of an idea what you are capable of, until the Lord gets a hold of you, but sometimes others see and want to decrease you. Only the Holy Spirit, who is Truth and full of power, can help you with your walk to make sure that your vision is birthed and manifested. Believe God and don't doubt His ability, He has the authority to bring it into fruition. When you start flowing in the anointing and blessings begin to come to pass, you will see whose whom, since the spirit of envy, jealousy, and covetousness is never far away.

Know your true purpose and be aware of the enemy!

## IN MY BELLY?

The Spirit of the Lord lives right inside the deepest part of your inner man where we call our stomach area, our belly. In 1980, we were living in the South Bronx, my mother and I were headed to my grandmother's house, and to my amazement I saw half of a man walking on his hands and waist. I've wondered how can a person live, and asking myself "Gee, where does the Holy Spirit dwell?" I remembered the text where it says—and I am paraphrasing—that the Spirit lives inside of your belly. "Out of your belly shall flow streams of living water." That was an awe moment for me when I was young, being ignorant to the fact that the Living Water *is* the Spirit of God. Your belly is also your heart, which is where you are, according to the New King James Version (John 7:38).

*The spirit of man is the candle of the LORD, searching all the **inward parts of the belly**.*
***Prov. 20:27** (KJV)* Emphasis added.

*He that believeth on me, as the scripture hath said, out of his **belly** shall flow rivers of living water.*
***John 7:38** (KJV)* Emphasis added.

## CAUTION!

At the age of eighteen I met a man who was twenty-eight years old who lived across the street from my mothers house. Knowing we moved on the block, he introduced himself to me saying he's a Muslim as well as inviting the neighbors to mosque and informing them about how inspirational his religion is. Eventually, the conversation ensued into a dialogue about Jesus' Spirit. Refusing to believe that there is a Spirit of God that lives inside of men by invitation, he would always change the subject in complete repudiation the Holy Spirit ever existed. As all Muslim's are known to do when I was growing up, they would constantly challenge the Lord's wisdom and knowledge from the passages of the Bible. The following day, he said to me plainly, "There is no Holy Spirit as you say." It really offended me since I felt he was trying to discredit the Spirit of Christ and my faith, which he would do constantly. Truthfully, he had the upper hand since he was well educated in both the Qu'ran and the Bible; the plight of it all, was the absolute fact he knew God's written Word better than I did. Apostle Peter said it best, "Be prepared always, to give an answer for the hope you have in Jesus," and I wasn't prepared.

*...But sanctify the Lord God in your hearts: and* **be ready always to give an answer to every man** *that asketh you a reason of the hope that is in you with meekness and fear...*
**1 Peter 3:15** *(KJV)* Emphasis added.

Eventually, as the months went by, I ended up falling into his traps as he baited me with the hottest music, feeding my ego, claiming I was one of the best rap artists in the city. Becoming Muslim was the end result of this whole entourage he had going on. Desiring to fit in, having the overwhelming feeling of being an important part of something worthy, I was willing to let go of Jesus after all the good His Spirit had shown me.

Hereafter, I remember their version of being born again called the Sha'jada or Shah'ada. It was totally different then what I have read in books. No Spirit of God comes to live in you, but a dark spirit of deception and militancy. Don't get me wrong I am not trying to attack Islam only sharing my testimony. I have met some very respectful and peaceful Muslims in mosque and in my community who were very rigid and firm. Apparently, most are not violent or troublesome in my experience, but as I began to study the Qu'ran and visiting the mosque, things started to change all together. Although, all Muslims are not terrorists, all terrorists as I see in the news are Muslim. Having that kind of information in my head didn't prevent me to keep on walking with this person whom I will call "Sean" (not his real name). He would always make sure everyday, coming into contact with the Spirit of God and fellowshipping with others in church, would not occur in my life. Demure in his speech and a smooth way of building his conniving words to make it seem so innocent and coy, he would always fool me, as I remember that day so clearly.

Seemingly so, it was like his destiny and assignment, was to make sure that I would not figure out what the devil was doing through him at all times. All the while living with my mother at the time, I would constantly be in his house for hours until dawn. Since he was a DJ, his house was the spot where all types of rap and R & B music would be played, with all his friends, relaxing and hanging out talking about Islam and other dark and idle topics.

One day my best friend Julio came with me to "Sean's" house, and we stayed all night until five in the morning making music, laughing, and talking. Whew! We were tired. Well after that visit "Sean" knew that my friend Julio, was a born again Christian. Consequently, as we spend time at his house, occasionally "Sean" would bash my friend Julio with his words for no apparent reason. This was going on for days, and days turned to weeks, and weeks, months. Every time Julio would go home early, "Sean" would badmouth him, His God, and Jesus. He believes that Jesus was a good man and a prophet, but at the same time talks bad about the Lord, always putting the Lord's name in vain. As I look back now, "Sean" and I walked in total confusion being blind to the devil's scheme and deceptive conduct causing my own downfall, with all of this happening to me in plain view for me to see. And yet, I did nothing to stop it knowing I was wrong and so was this pagan religion.

# DRIFTED

I started fading away further and further from the church and other believers. I began to drift heavy into Islam at full force without a care in the world where I was headed. As time went on, part of me was looking forward to visit the mosque with "Sean," and at the same time, noticing my attitude was spinning out of control on an entire different level of distorted thinking. I started talking back to my mother and disrespecting my younger brothers consistently. Suddenly, a hatred for Caucasian people started rising up within me. Then the hatred was targeting everyone around me, and eventually hating myself. Not noticing at that time, I remember people looked different to me; it was really creeping me out and scaring me, and yet, I kept going to mosque. In service, I met the Imam (teacher), one of the facilitators of the service and teacher of the Qu'ran. The Imam spoke to me about the five books of Islam, saying I needed to purchase all five of those books. He reached over to a table behind him near the library by the counter and showed me a different book with a picture of a Caucasian doctor delivering a white baby, with small horns and a pointed tail. The Imam said, "This is the reason why we call whites, blue eye devils." Now keep in mind, this experience doesn't mean that all mosques are the same, or that Imams are equal in their teachings, this was my own experience. Four months have passed since I started visiting these services, leaving the Lord and passionately analyzing the Qu'ran was my focus. I no longer had an interest for the Bible, and I pushed it to the side getting ready to dump it. For some reason something within me would not let me throw the Bible away in the garbage, and yet I would not pick it up and read it. Attending mosque and reading the "Qu'ran" and the "Fur'qan al Haq" (one of the five books of Islam) was more important to me then attending church and reading a Bible from a white man's God and religion, compared to Allah. The knowledge of Islam meaning submission began to over flood my mind with distorted views of how I saw Jesus and white people. When my mother would cook meat I would make sure pork was not in any of my food because I thought the white man was trying to control and destroy my mind. This is one of the teachings of the Koran or Qu'ran.

One evening while watching television in the living room my mother entered and said, "Luis, I know lately you have been hanging out with "Sean," and I don't like it." "I over heard him talking to you about me, if you think for a second you are going to listen to him and try to tell me off, when I correct you, or even bad mouth me, you will have to move out of my house." "I am your mother you are to honor me!" I felt so small, and embarrassed I went to my room and didn't come out until the next day. While all of this was going on, Julio had no clue that in my heart he became my enemy. As I was getting ready for bed my room felt weird, I paid no mine and went to sleep and started to have these terrible dreams. Demons were visiting me in my sleep giving me nightmares, and I remember the feeling of not being able to come out of my dream. Once I became aware of what was happening to me I tried to come out of it, and I couldn't. Physically I was trying to yell out, Jesus! They would cover my mouth. (Notice I didn't call out Allah or Mohammed). Finally, I came to myself, yelling out Jesus' name and those repulsive spirits left.

## JESUS, IS THAT YOU?

A few nights later, after hanging out with "Sean" I went home, prayed to Allah, and fell asleep. I had a second dream, and this dream felt so real and supernatural it amazes me even now, like it happened just yesterday. I really thought everything that happened in this dream was occurring for real; it was a very scaring feeling, worse then demonic spirits attacking you. In the dream I saw myself in the morning getting out of bed, and I walked out of my house, on the right side of the cement porch to the front doorsteps I paused for a moment, and looked around. It was a beautiful day. The street I lived on looked exactly as it did in real life. Unexpectedly, a loud noise thundered in the first heaven—the sky. I see from the corner of my eye, an image, I made a complete turn to have a better look, and about the height where a plane would fly, a huge man in all white was walking toward Julio's house. The angel's height was a little shorter then the man, and they were bouncing behind Him leaping for joy, walking and passing me by like I didn't exist. Immediately what came into my mind was, "Whoa! This is Jesus! This is the rapture, this is the end!" I started to run eastward down my street yelling in a loud voice, Jesus! Jesus! Don't forget me! He simply ignored me like I wasn't even there. This dream felt so corporeal it was phenomenal; it really felt like it was literally happening in real life. I kept waving my hands running with all that was in me toward Him saying, "Jesus don't forget me, it's me Luis! It's me! It's me!" He kept on walking and the angels paid me no mind to me even still. My cries fell on deaf ears. An unexplainable fear began to overtake me. This fear was Holy! When the fear of the Lord falls on you, it pushes you down to your knees especially when you are not right with God. This fear was causing my knees to buckle and I became very weak. Thereafter, I was violently pushed out of my dream with tremendous force and my heart started racing really fast.

That morning when I awoke, before my mind can catch up to the fact that I was up, if that makes sense, I heard the Lord's voice say, "Go!" I knew exactly what that meant. I made haste and got dressed running straight to Julio's house, covering about two blocks in less than five minutes. Knocking at his door like a madman and out of breath, Tada! Julio opens the front door. I did not know he knew about all the garbage "Sean" and I were saying about him. I said to him,

"Julio, I'm so sorry for what I have done to you, I didn't mean to talk bad and starting false rumors about you, I don't know what came over me. Can you still be my friend?" "Do you forgive me?" "I am so sorry." He replied, "I forgave you when I first heard you were talking bad about me." When he said that, I broke out into tears. The love of Christ was deep in his heart; it cut me like a knife through my soul and spirit. Expecting him to hate me and give me in return what I gave him, was my expectation, and he proved me wrong, and we hugged. Ever since the dream and that day at Julio's parent's house, the spirits that were holding me down broke off of me. When God spoke to me it shattered the strong man that was controlling me immediately. The chains of spiritual blindness and bondage of tortuous lies exploded into flames in the spirit, instantly! In all the months serving Allah, not once I read anything about he loves his children or that he died for me, you will not find it in any of the surah's, which are chapters in the Qu'ran. He is not to be considered as a Father or having children neither, there is no love that I have found throughout the entire surah's of the Qu'ran. Not once, when I had a very critical need or was experiencing hard problems, he spoke to me and let me know everything is going to be ok. The devil is a liar! I never did go back to "Sean's" house again. As I said before, every wolf has paws, check there feet, the devil is under it, check there feet; it is not beautiful nor brings good news.

*The **steps** of a good man are ordered by the Lord, and He delights in his way.*
**Psalms 37:23** *(NKJV)* Emphasis added.

*How beautiful are the **feet** of those who preach the gospel of peace, who bring glad tidings of good things!"*
**Romans 10:15** *(NKJV)* Emphasis added.

I was totally made free! Although, "Sean" looked for me I made sure my availability to him was lost. Eventually, that friendship starved and died. I spoke death to that terrible relationship, it really needed to die and stay dead. The anointing breaks the yoke of bondage. We all must learn from each other. We need each other on a daily basis. Wolves, and counterfeit Christians, come in like manner, kind, gentle, and understanding at first, but their agenda is to kill you!

## WAKE UP!

Makes no difference where you are in the world reading this book, as long as you have a voice and a body with breath, it is never too late to get it right with Jesus. Do not condemn yourself by your own standards, the sin might be terrible and maybe very great, but when He sees His Son's blood, which was shed on the cross, is much greater than you could ever imagine. When a man or woman says, that Jesus and His shed blood on Calvary was a stupid idea or they reject that kind of love, in reality it's like smacking God in His face. It's like telling the Lord, (scoffing) "Hmph! Is this what you sent to earth to die for me, a man named Jesus, He is not worth it?" When the unbeliever controverts against the Lord, they are **demon**strating what God gave us to die in our benefit as something hollow, obscure, and not good enough, a waste of time. Wake up people! The time of the end is upon us; we must worship God in His spirit and in His truth. Jesus' death on the cross is none of these wicked things, but the power of God, manifested for all to see and accept with a contrite and broken spirit of surrender to His will.

Do not harden your hearts from the one who paid such a high price.

*Today, if you will hear His voice: Do not harden your hearts, as in the rebellion, As in the day of trial in the wilderness*
**Psalms 95:7-8** *(NKJV).*

*Therefore, as the Holy Spirit says: "Today, if you will hear His voice, do not harden your hearts as in the rebellion, In the day of trial in the wilderness…*
**Heb. 3:7-8** *(NKJV)*

The Holy Spirit is waiting on you Sister.

The Holy Spirit is waiting on you Brother.

God has His arms wide open to receive you totally and completely. Torn down and broken inside or on the outside, makes no bit a difference with the Lord. Let him who stole, steal no more, let him who gossiped, gossip no more. The Almighty Savior is waiting for you.

If you are already saved, I ask you these questions and answer yourself truthfully.

"Can people tell you are saved?"

"Can others see that milk and honey resides in the atmosphere of your heart?"

"Do they feel the land of promise overcoming them with your humility and overflowing meekness?"

"Do they feel offended or distant from you every time you leave their presence?"

Beloved, if you have some negative dealings weighing you down in your mind and your spirit, I encourage you right now to put your thoughts down on paper. Pray over them, as you represent it to God, it would be a good time to do that right now. This will be your time to meditate over those issues and give it to God; the burden is too much for you to carry. To the men, I hearten you to take a moment and reflect truly what you might need to note down, to help you pray against what might be holding you back from confessing to God, and forsaking whatever it is you are dealing with. I always see women reflect, and on rare occasions the men, so I implore anyone reading this book to write *it* down and make it plain for you and God to see. Lets do it! In Jesus name, lets bind that thing and loose His freedom and promises into our lives like a cascade.

*And I will give you the keys of the kingdom of heaven, and whatever you bind on earth will be bound in heaven, and whatever you loose on earth will be loosed in heaven.*
**Matt. 16:19** *(NKJV)*

*Assuredly, I say to you, whatever you bind on earth will be bound in heaven, and whatever you loose on earth will be loosed in heaven.*
**Matt. 18:18** *(NKJV)*

*Write the vision and make it plain on tablets, that he may run who reads it. For the vision is yet for an appointed time, but at the end it will speak, and it will not lie. Though it tarries, wait for it, because it will surely come, it will not tarry.*
**Habakkuk 2:2-3** *(NKJV)*

# HEARTFELT MEDITATIONS

_____

_____

_____

_____

_____

_____

_____

_____

_____

_____

_____

_____

_____

_____

_____

_____

_____

_____

_____

_____

_____

_____

_____

*This Book of the Law shall not depart from your mouth, but you shall* **meditate** *in it day and night, that you may observe to do according to all that is written in it. For then you will make your way prosperous, and then you will have good success.*
**Joshua 1:8** *(NKJV)* Emphasis added.

*Let the words of my mouth and the* **meditation** *of my heart be acceptable in Your sight, O* LORD, *my strength and my Redeemer.*
**Psalms 19:14** *(NKJV)* Emphasis added.

Have you forgotten the old saying, "sinners run from God, and saints run to God?" You always must be in a mindset of total surrender, walking in His Faith (Hebrews 11:6). In order to accomplish freedom and truth, you must stay away from these attributes and characteristics that can cause you to fall along the lines of becoming a carnal and a counterfeit Christian, especially when you have no intention to change for the better. Nevertheless, hold your ground and war against the pessimistic and demonic inspired elements set before you by your adversary.

- Adultery
- Accusation
- Apathy
- Backbiting
- Backsliding
- Bitterness
- Complacency
- Contention
- Debauchery
- False humility
- Fantasy lust
- Fits of rage
- Gossip
- Gluttony
- Greed
- Hate
- Haughty spirit
- Idolatry
- Loose living
- Lukewarmness
- Lust
- Lying
- Pride
- Rebellion
- Sexual immorality
- Strife
- Theft
- Uncontrolled anger

- Unforgiveness
- Witchcraft

And the list goes on and on...heed to RED FLAGS...Stay away from exercising this list the best you can. In case you are struggling with what is listed above, I encourage you to pray to the Lord and be totally real with Him, and if you need help call someone you can trust, who is a strong believer in the Lord. There is nothing worse than someone who walks in the office of hypocrisy and artificiality.

*Confess your trespasses to one another, and pray for one another, that you may be healed. The effective, fervent prayer of a righteous man avails much.*
**James 5:16** *(NKJV)*

Let's all come to the conclusion of bowing our heads to a God who desires to be worshipped and praised. Make it your goal to live life day by day in the authority and virtue of the Holy Spirit. Allowing the fruit of the Spirit to resonate in your members, being vigorous for the kingdom always, with the attitude and sincerity of worshipping Him in Spirit and in Truth.

CHAPTER SEVEN

# KNOCK. KNOCK. WHO IS IT?
# L.U.S.T.

# Chapter Seven

==========

# KNOCK. KNOCK.
## WHO IS IT?
### L.U.S.T.

*I say then: walk in the Spirit, and you shall not fulfill the lust of the flesh. For the flesh lusts against the Spirit, and the Spirit against the flesh, and these are contrary to one another, so that you do not do the things that you wish.*

**—Galatians 5:16-17**

*For the grace of God that brings salvation has appeared to all men, teaching us that, denying ungodliness and worldly lusts, we should live soberly, righteously, and godly in the present age...*
**—Titus 2:11-12**

As WE KEEP LIVING LIFE and develop into becoming older, we grow to be encircled with all diverse kinds of temptations. The believer has to become prepared and equipped when *Lust* and *Fantasy Lust* come your way. *Lust* is defined in two different ways:

1. Strong sexual and sensual desire toward someone other than yourself

2. Intense longing for something (*like power and control*)

My acronym for *Lust*:

**L.**UST   **U.**NIFIES   **S.**EX   &   **T.**EMPTATIONS

As we study the sacred Word of the Lord, you will come to notice from Genesis to Revelation, lust is not merely sexual. Lust is also linked to a person's evil desire and greed in adherence to materialism, and self-gratification. Scripture tells us that we must come against and cast down these kinds of thoughts and actions in our everyday living.

Consequently, its association with sexual behaviors has been amplified in the church, and the world. Lust is not only executing and slipping its ways of perversion in the house of the Lord, but also in society everywhere. Pornography is destroying lives, homes, and marriages, which are falling apart by the second. The divorce rate with Christians is surpassing the divorce rate of the world's matrimonies. Now this spirit is overflowing into our young people, the saved, and unsaved, the churchgoer, and the non-churchgoer. They all are arriving in an arena, knowing they will never return from their fornications and wicked deeds, chiefly if their conscience is seared. The Lord God has designed His expressions very clear since the beginning of time, to make sure we stay away from *all* kinds of sensual, sexual, and lustful sins. Lust, is held in a high regard as one of the deadliest of our sinful nature alongside debauchery. On the basis when lust and debauchery are united, it contains the power to open you up to various fiend spirits, imps, demons, pornography, and Belial. These spirits have the power spiritually and physically to overpower you, causing mental slavery. Only the Holy Spirit and the anointing can break the back of despotism over your life. Exposition with any of these malicious spirits—and they do work as a team—you would need a minister anointed with a powerful deliverance ministry, to assist in breaking the cycle of any generational curse, and familiar spirits that you may have invited into your inner circle. Deliverance is needed in order to be set free from these types of strongholds; this is very vital in the life of the believer.

*But every man is tempted, when he is drawn away of his own lust, and enticed. Then when lust hath conceived, it bringeth forth sin: and sin, when it is finished, bringeth forth death.*
**James 1:14-15** *(KJV)*

*You must understand this: In the last days there will be violent periods of time. People will be selfish and love money. They will brag, be arrogant, and use abusive language. They will curse their parents, show no gratitude, have no respect for what is holy, and lack normal affection for their families. They will refuse to make peace with anyone. They will be slanderous, lack self-control, be brutal, and have no love for what is good. They will be traitors. They will be reckless and conceited. They will love pleasure rather than God. They will appear to have a godly life, but they will not let its power change them. Stay away from such people.*
**2 Tim. 3:1-5** *(Gods Word)*

*Their minds are corrupt, and the faith they teach is counterfeit.*
**2 Tim. 3:8** *(Gods Word)*

This enticement of wantonness is very powerful, like a drug, it takes you into a world of false hopes and dreams. Society as a whole is collapsing right in front of us and we have no idea how to stop it. But we serve a God who holds everything in the power of His Name.

First, war against it with the spirit of prayer.

Secondly, defeat the enemy by not taking part of his false endeavors.

Thirdly, fast for what is good, and abstain from evil desires of all sorts.

The lifestyle of promiscuity and distorted views of how sex is supposed to be portrayed is at the moment running this great country of ours down to total destruction–in the natural as well in the spiritual. Corrupt mentalities, combined with strong lustful envy has boosted an impish culture consumed in the dominion of pornography, evolving it into a multi-billion dollar a year industry, surpassing alcohol and drugs combined. Lechery is a powerful weapon we have pursued in our flesh and soul without giving ear to the many consequences, which are very significant in the construct of our culture. Even as the years have gone by, the church no longer speaks about these issues because of the explicit nature and graphic content it contains. However, it is so critical in the days we are living in (Hosea 4:6). Saints have to be transformed mentally according to the well-timed Scriptures the apostle Paul wrote about in Romans.

*I beseech you therefore, brethren, by the mercies of God, that you **present your bodies** a living sacrifice, **holy**, acceptable to God, which is your reasonable service. And **do not be conformed to this world**, but be **transformed by the renewing of your mind**, that you may prove what is that good and acceptable and perfect will of God.* **Romans 12:1-2** *(NKJV)* Emphasis added.

## SPIRITUAL SUICIDE

Demons do not force you to fall into the hands of a Jezebel spirit; you invite it in by a willing heart. Sometimes you would hear believers say, "The devil made me do it." or "I couldn't help it, the temptation was just too strong to fight off." Somewhere along those lines you would hear these excuses, but it's a fine line between an excuse and a person who is willing to sin. Reality tells me they themselves were the one listening and entertaining the images and thoughts, that entered into the theatre of their minds, without taking into consideration that he or she was suppose to cast those iniquitous mental movies down. If an image comes into your mind, you have less than three seconds to cast it down before it gets to your heart. Once it gets into your soul's heart it is too late, you are already ensnared by your wicked deceitfulness of your own desire.

*The **heart is deceitful** above all things, and **desperately wicked**: who can know it?*
***Jer. 17:9** (KJV)* Emphasis added.

***Casting down imaginations**, and every high thing that exalteth itself against the knowledge of God, and bringing into captivity every thought to the obedience of Christ; and having in a readiness to revenge all disobedience, when your obedience is fulfilled.*
***2 Cor. 10:5-6** (KJV)* Emphasis added.

## LUST OF THE FLESH

Nowhere in Scripture, would you find a spirit of lust (James 1:14) and (Romans 6:12). In James it says, "...but every man is tempted when he is drawn away of his *own* lust and enticed." Enticed means to: attract with pleasure and reward. Written by the apostles to caution the Body of Christ, was to instruct how not to allow sin to reign in our mortal bodies that we should obey it in the lust thereof. For all that is in the world the lust of the flesh, lust of the eyes, and the pride of life, is not of the Father, but of the world (1 John 2:16). Fifty Scripture references never state lust is a demonic spirit. It's our own lust we must bring into subjection to God's Holy Word, every day. Fighting with Scripture feedback, consecration, quotes of warfare, prayer, and fasting is the key to this entire ordeal. Lust open doors to the general evil spirit named *Belial*, all kinds of perverted spirits are under his authority. He sends them to tempt you, but there is no spirit that goes in you to force you to fall into sin, unless invited or willing. Distorted sexual views and openness will unlock portals that will be hard to close. It will physically and spiritually destroy you and keep you longer than you ever intended. When it is done with you, you are dead! We must fall on our faces in the sight of God in these evil days, as it gets darker and darker by the minute. Notice all the movies and television shows, with vulgar word's being said that were never allowed when I was a kid, are now televised with no conscience. Sex and vulgarity have been and are being amplified, exhibited with graphic visuals that need to be filtered, so our kids don't hear and see the perversion of the world's social disorder. The Lord has made a way for the Christian to take the Word of God to run with zeal for the Good News of Christ to protect our moral values we have left. Take holiness and purity by force immediately, or you will stumble before the King of Kings. As a living sacrifice you have to deny yourself Christian, when it comes to evil desires and wants. The Spirit of the Lord will help and guide you, **if** you call on His Name. We are living in a desperate and chaotic age, but God has a plan to redeem and refresh us all in the near future. Hanging on to what is good is the duty of all those who are saved and Holy Ghost filled. We must endure until the end and fight with wisdom for us to experience the refreshing that is coming. Be ready always and fight your flesh until the end, and you will be rewarded.

*Therefore let him who thinks he stands take heed lest he fall. No temptation has overtaken you except such as is common to man; but God is faithful, who will not allow you to be tempted beyond what you are able, but with the temptation will also make the way of escape, that you may be able to bear it.*
**1 Cor. 10:12-13** *(NKJV)*

Authentic Christians must want the relief only Christ can give for them to walk in liberty. The Holy Spirit will then see you are serious. He burns like a fire within your members. Captivating your inner mind and soul with piety making you complete and whole on the inside. He causes you to put a halt on your cravings that are contradictory to God's laws and His mental map of holiness so you can walk in His freedom.

## KNOCK. KNOCK. WHO IS IT? LUST

"Worship warrior,"

"Spiritual Successor,"

"Power Praiser,"

"Obedient Servant" of the Lord, is who you are!

It's Christ who rewards you openly, operating, and satisfying the empty and the fallen.

Feeling like a failure but yet successful. Having conflict and disruption on all sides, and yet you have a battle cry on reserve. Saints adjust yourself and be prepared; lust will constantly knock on the door of your heart, when it does knock you have to let it knock and never answer.

To the singles who are sexually frustrated, you must go above and beyond what is expected of you. Jesus will always be there to give you the strength that you need enabling you to do all things through Him (Philippians 4:8, 9, 13). Depend on God, with all of your might! *"Be strong in the Lord and in the power of His might"* Ephesians 6:10. *"…Not by might, nor by power, but by My Spirit says the Lord of hosts"* Zechariah 4:6.

Nevertheless, the Lord will be His Name forever! A King who will reign eternally is His decree and mannerism from everlasting to everlasting. Ad-infinitum belongs to our God, after dissecting the plans of the enemy to know your true purpose in your life, infinity will not be given to you if you fall in the company of evil desires and camp there. Goodness and mercy, is your stepping-stone traveling with you throughout your years. I tried to amend myself with my authority, purportedly setting myself free; unknowingly the freedom from bondage was by the influence of Jesus' Spirit. Now I know to take comfort in His existence, which is above all. As a righteous man who encounters concupiscence, he must learn to deflect lust by the influence of God's Spirit of purity to resist depraved ambitions, whether sexual or not. Surround yourself in the midst of the Lord above; a salacious spirit will be subject to the Spirit of Christ, which could never co-exist when sitting on the right side of the Throne of Power in your heart! All born again believers who have their name written in the Lambs Book of Life are seated in heavenly places. Glory to God!

*Many are the afflictions of the righteous, but the* LORD *delivers him out of them all.*
**Psalms 34:19** *(NKJV)*

*Therefore submit to God.* **Resist** *the devil and he will flee from you. Draw near to God and He will draw near to you…*
**James 4:7-8** *(NKJV)* Emphasis added.

*...Raised us up together, and made us sit together in the heavenly places in Christ Jesus, that in the ages to come He might show the exceeding riches of His grace in His kindness toward us in Christ Jesus.*
**Eph. 2:6-7** *(NKJV)*

# A KING WITH A SECRET

Lust was a downfall for one of the greatest Kings that ever walked the face of the earth, King David the prophet of the Great YAHWEH. King David watched **Bath**sheeba as she was taking a **Bath** from his palace. To the extreme point of giving into lechery and yearning for her, made her pregnant. Afterward, he contemplated within himself how would he kill Bathsheeba's husband, Uriah the Hittite, so he could have her. Using his power ineptly fed the dark endless abyss of his own lust, misusing his power and authority to deceive in order to get what he wickedly desired. When he did receive what he craved, it was more than he could bear. I am sure he has learned his lesson, but I noticed reading the Psalms it was a very difficult trail to walk on.

# LUST FOR REPUTATION AND RICHES

Samson and Delilah is an account in the Bible of betrayal between two consenting adults, engulfed with unequal passion of burning desire one to another for the wrong reasons. Samson lusted after her beauty and Delilah lusted after greed and obsession for 1,100 pieces of silver. Read Judges Chapter 16.

## SATAN, THE GREAT COUNTERFEITER

Needless to say, the Bible points out countless others who fell in a similar snare for voracity and control. Nonetheless, God has proven Himself faithful to all of His servants by modifying their lives into something great. On the basis of knocking the devil off of his platform of pride, and obliterating him, from driving the people of God into nothingness. **Caution:** As you know, Satan is the great counterfeiter; he will mimic his way into every tiny crack available to him, with the goal of making sure you follow hard after him to cohere pride and false worship into your life and your surroundings.

## THE WORK IS NEVER DONE

You will read throughout the writings of the prophets, all the troubles they had to face and come in contact with, and still held on to what was good for the Will of God. You will discover as you compare recorded events in the past with real life events of today, you will see equivalent topics that have been going on since the very beginning. Perpetually, egotistic concepts and ideas even in our time with the notion that there is still nothing new under the sun, makes Solomon's writings come alive in our lifetime. Pacing yourself into 'The Hands' of victory will be challenging at first, and yet, rewarding in the end as He continues to mold you. Nevertheless, after He takes you out of the fire and you are looking beautiful, even then He is not done with you. The work always continues until your change comes. God's ways are so divergent, He desires for you to be transformed by the renewing of your mind with the anticipation of staying that way. Transformation is necessary to help you affray against the traps of Satan, the lusts of your flesh and the world.

On the other hand, those who say that God is understanding of our wallowing in sin, that He will not allow judgment to be executed on your life, is only self-deceived. Here is a warning that apostle Paul wrote to the people of Galatia. Galatians 5:16 assert, *"Walk in the spirit and you will not fulfill the lust of the flesh."* From Genesis to Revelation you will always read about, "the lust of the flesh" not of the spirit(s), and the damage it has caused all through history. Christ and the apostles understood this to the very core, apostle Paul expressed this in Romans Chapter 7:14-21 in detail of his personal struggles while being single. The other apostles, who wrote the gospels, in plain speculation, were single, and maybe remained that way throughout the entire course of their ministry, or, maybe married afterward.

## CALL NO MAN FATHER?

Lust, whether spiritual, soulish, or natural in your eyes, is sin in the eyes of Christ. Consider this carefully: When you have a man who is called "father" after Jesus said, "Call no man father," He was not telling us not to call our dad, father; He was discussing this with a different audience, which I believe He foreknew that Catholicism would arise after He ascended back to His heavenly Father. Now, a priest that is called "father" would go into one side of the booth and those who practice the religion of Catholicism would know to enter the same booth on the other side. A dialogue ensues with private confessions of all types of sinful activities the individual have committed, stating, "Father forgive me for I have sinned." After years and years of known and unknown members confessing their sins to the priest, a transformation begins to take place in the atmosphere, and in the spirit of that man, most times unknowingly. Having one man listening into the ear gate of his soul with years of ill admission and vulgar behavior can destroy a life in many ways quickly. Why

I say this? Lets look at it from another point of view. Jesus plainly said–and I'm paraphrasing. "Don't confess your sins to mere men, because he is just that, a man. He doesn't have the authority or the supremacy to forgive you, nor is he able to wash your sins away and repel the weight of sin." Ponder what Jesus said, because it makes total and complete sense. Confessing all kinds of sins, lies, lust issues, and everything under the sun you can think of, will put a 'father' or 'priest' to his knees opening portals to satanic oppression. (Keep in mind most Catholic priests are not born again Christians). Here is the turn around and affect of this religious process; in amazement we see them on the news for molestation, rape, or sodomy charges, sometimes all of the above. It's rare you see a pastor or a prophet on the news for such crimes. I am sure somewhere in our country and in our world it's happening, we are not to be naïve of that fact, but it's not as frequent and televised. If a pastor or anyone in ministry is guilty of the same behavior in the presence of Christ, you better believe it will not go unpunished, even if its not televised or in the morning paper.

We have the Holy Spirit to convict us and guide us, allowing us to be married, so our minds do not travel further than our flesh should go. Sadly, the priest or father gets either expelled or excluded out of the Vatican or the Catholic Church. When you come to the conclusion of the filth a "father" from a Catholic religion has been going through, listening to the heaviness of sin, a priest doesn't have the capability to be able to contain and maintain a pure heart and mind before God. The heart is so deceitfully wicked how can anyone understand or know it (Jeremiah 17:9). Why? Sin is a great burden to carry on anyone's shoulder. The end result is you act out what has been poured into you. Countless priests and fathers keeping themselves from women and having different people from all walks of life, visiting and confessing month after month and year after year their sexual immoralities, eventually will take a hold on them sexually. The sins of men are to heavy for a mere mortal man to deal with. God has created us to be sexual beings, but in the confines of marriage and not fornication and promiscuity. Lust is very powerful especially when you feed it. Essentially, we all understand that not everyone will act on every thought or devious behavior, but we all must be clever to know the designs of the devil and how he is trying to destroy us. Be aware of the enemy and know your true purpose. Apostle Paul addressed this in 1 Corinthians chapter 7 and Ephesians chapter 4.

*…If they cannot exercise self-control, let them marry. For it is better to marry than to burn with passion.*
***1 Cor. 7:9*** *(NKJV)*

*This I say, therefore, and testify in the Lord, that you should no longer walk as the rest of the Gentiles walk, in the futility of their mind, having their understanding darkened, being alienated from the life of God, because of the ignorance that is in them, because of the blindness of their heart; who, being past feeling, have given themselves over to lewdness, to work all uncleanness with greediness. But you have not so learned Christ, if indeed you have heard Him and have been taught by Him, as the truth is in Jesus: that you put off, concerning your former conduct, the old man which grows corrupt according to the deceitful lusts, and be renewed in the spirit of your mind, and that you put on the new man which was created according to God, in true righteousness and holiness.*
***Eph. 4:17-24*** *(NKJV)*

## LUST FOR POSITION AND POWER

To consider Peter as the first Pope, has confused millions of people, knowing Popes have no dealings with women or marriage, and yet Peter had a mother-in-law, the only way you would have a mother-in-law, is if you are married to the daughter. It goes to show how people take the Scriptures to another level, causing contexts to become ploy and taking the true character and nature out of the attributes of the Word, and misconstrue what the Lord was trying to relay to mankind. Misinterpretation is a very powerful arsenal if we are not careful. This coincides in the same characteristics of Christianity and the Bible.

We misinterpret the signs of sexual promiscuity and perversion. Brother or Sister I say again, you have to be wise beyond your years, read your Bible and spend lots of time with God in prayer. Think of prayer as **P**owerful **R**esources **A**t **Y**our **E**arliest **R**equest

*Be anxious for nothing, but in everything by prayer and supplication, with thanksgiving,* **let your requests be made known to God***; and the peace of God, which surpasses all understanding, will guard your hearts and minds through Christ Jesus.*
**Phil. 4:6-7** *(NKJV)* Emphasis added.


## SATAN, SIN, AND SEDUCTION


The one thing I can truly say with certainty is that there is victory if you keep up with the obedience of willingness to follow hard after God, despite the problems stirring in the very apex of your intelligence. Many of us know better and we still keep dabbing into sin and its nature. Saints this should not be so. Consecrate yourselves and give your all to the Lord Jesus Christ without turning back, like Ado, the wife of Lot, when she turned into a pillar of salt. She looked back, and that was a metaphoric sign of, "I don't want to start afresh I miss my old life." Violating the passage when, *"Jesus said to him, "No one, having put his hand to the plow, and looking back, is fit for the kingdom of God."* Luke 9:62. The leading of the Spirit of Christ and allowing yourself to be led you will make it. I encourage you to let a friend, a sister, and a brother, saved or unsaved know that they could make it as long as they have the Spirit of Life within them. Satan is a liar and the father of it. Whether you lust after material things, control, authority, power, or sexual pleasures, unless it's taken care of quickly, you will be shaken and shattered. Believers must adhere to the Word, and the Lord's commandments and stay away from Satan's craftiness when he releases snares to captivate you with impious seductions. Personally, I have seen worldly people right along with Christians fall on their face quickly; other times slowly, the devil will make sure of that, guaranteed! Evil spirits know who you are and if you are really serving the Lord or just being counterfeit. They are very daring and will expose you to whoever is around you.

*Now God worked unusual miracles by the hands of Paul, so that even handkerchiefs or aprons were brought from his body to the sick, and the diseases left them and the evil spirits went out of them. Then some of the itinerant Jewish exorcists took it upon themselves to call the name of the Lord Jesus over those who had evil spirits, saying, "We exorcise you by the Jesus whom Paul preaches." Also there were seven sons of Sceva, a Jewish chief priest, who did so. And the evil spirit answered and said, "Jesus I know, and Paul I know; but who are you?" Then the man in whom the evil spirit was leaped on them, overpowered them, and prevailed against them, so that they fled out of that house naked and wounded.*
**Acts 19:11-16** *(NKJV)*

Image Bearer, if you take this for banter, demons will have a field day in your thought life. They will bombard you with all kinds of miscellaneous temptations; graphic images will be displayed in your mind to knock you off track. It is true as I mentioned earlier, when the Bible says, where the Spirit of the Lord is there is freedom. Commit to memory when the Son makes you free, you are free indeed, because the anointing breaks the yoke of bondage. There is a big difference between being *set free* and *made free*. Allow me to paint a picture with the differences between the two.

Being *Set Free* is when you have an inmate locked up in a jail cell, gets released and yet he is still behind bars in pure bondage in his heart, mind, and spirit even while his body is experiencing freedom.

Being *Made Free*, he receives Christ as Lord and Savior, he will experience liberty whether locked behind bars or not, for the reason that the anointing destroys the yoke of mental and spiritual slavery. This allows anyone to experience genuine freedom with joy. This is true liberation of Christ. So lets all walk audaciously and not weaken.

*Now the Lord is the Spirit; and where the Spirit of the Lord is, there is liberty.*
**2 Cor. 3:17** *(NKJV)*

*Therefore if the Son makes you free, you shall be free indeed.*
**John 8:36** *(NKJV)*

## DECEPTIVE DESIRES

In all of this, I ask you to pray that the Body of Christ would understand the precise characteristics of the Son of Man who walked a short journey with his soul and body, but made camp in the Spirit. The campfire of the Lord is magnificent and Holy unable to be explained in finite language. We must make Jesus' ways known. Allowing lust and its relatives reside in your members is not a wise choice to make. From my point of view and comprehension of lust, will take you to places that would be impossible to return. I never drank or did drugs, but

I tell you the truth, this was my drug and it was bad. Trouble after trouble, marching slowly in a desert of counterfeit desires, will kill you! Chiefly, it will always want more and more, "Just one more look," or "Just one more second." Those thoughts are all deceptions of the flesh and the devil, with his bow in hand playing archery contests in your mind, seeing who will win, you or him. If you are a man, you know a man's troubles are many; but it's the Lord who delivers him out of them all. Earlier in the book I mentioned briefly about thoughts and how to encounter them and the intricacies that follow after. Please take heed to it for it is your life on the line.

## ON SECOND THOUGHT

Let me start by saying, Jesus spoke about His sheep knowing His voice. Essentially, this is very true to the essence. Thoughts are very translucent and vague at times, but mostly enlightening. Allow me to explain what I mean. Not every thought that invites itself into your mental soul is yours. Having discernment and wisdom is very critical in the Christians life with the inclination of the Spirit, to assist and counter attack evil thoughts with the Word. When a thought rises up into your mind, sometimes it's just you; other times it's your enemy with his fiery darts penetrating, causing the person to be interrupted and disrupted in their thought process. Picture the factor when the Bible says, flaming or fiery darts since they are considered burning and heated thoughts. Let's say the thought was a negative one. You will always hear the right thought voice speak to you first, then the wrong one enters immediately right after. It's just the second 'thought voice' sounds much louder than the original. The second thought is always the one that wants you to do an act of evil or say something that is unfruitful and not accepted in the ears of God or the individual. The first contradicts the second on a regular basis. As these thoughts go in and out of your mind, you need to discern them quickly and wisely, if it exalts itself against the knowledge of God and His Word, cast it down immediately. We have seen hundreds maybe thousands of men and women, even children act out on their thoughts and the results were clearly devastating. I say that the Bible is the greatest sleeping pill. How come? The minute you begin to read it to purify your mind from dissimilar class of imagery, all of a sudden a spirit of slumber interrupts you causing your body to yawn leading you to feel tired and sleepy. I say to that believer to stand up and do a few jumping jacks or have a drink of water and you will feel refreshed and renewed, this is how you know it's a spirit of slumber making you sleepy. Multitudes of believers in these last days can tell the difference if it's God or the Devil talking to them. Your thought voice is your own, be scrupulous at all times.

*For I know the thoughts that I think toward you, says the LORD, thoughts of peace and not of evil, to give you a future and a hope.*
***Jer. 29:11 (NKJV)***

In essence, you have to be aware of the content and what kind of information that is being deposited into you. Saints must know how to become one with God and learn to hear His still small voice, so when The Shepherd speaks there is no confusion in the process. Prophets or Prophetesses of God, like my wife Michelle, hears the Holy Spirit's voice most of the time audibly on the outside, and occasionally from the inside. Rarely she feels impressed in her spirit when God speaks or says that God laid this or that on her heart, actually she literally hears His still small voice which is not my wife's own thought voice, that is awesome! I say that to say this, re-tune and quiet yourself away from all the noise that surrounds you...and the Lord will speak to you.

*Then He said, "Go out, and stand on the mountain before the* Lord.*"*
*And behold, the* Lord *passed by, and a great and strong wind tore into the*
*mountains and broke the rocks in pieces before the* Lord, *but the* Lord
*was not in the wind; and after the wind an earthquake, but the* Lord was
*not in the earthquake; and after the earthquake a fire, but the* Lord *was*
*not in the fire; and after the fire **a still small voice**. So it was, when*
*Elijah heard it, that he wrapped his face in his mantle and went out and*
*stood in the entrance of the cave. **Suddenly a voice came to him**,*
*and said, "What are you doing here, Elijah?"*
***1 Kings 19:11-13** (NKJV)* Emphasis added.

We are no different or better than you or anyone else.
You don't need a title in order to hear the awesomeness of
His voice. One thing you do need is an ear to hear what the
Spirit is saying to the church, YOU! God is always speaking
and yet not a blabbermouth. The Great Architect desires
to converse with His children, at the same time, the devil
also wants to converse with his children and the children
of God. He uses your own thought voice so you could be
swindled making it extremely difficult to determine whose
speaking to you. If the devil uses his supernatural voice, a
human being will flip and go crazy, because of the way his
voice would sound, this will blow his cover and prevents
you from implementing what he instructed. Therefore, he
gets frustrated when unable to carry out his plan through the
individual from performing what was programmed into the
person, revealing his trickery. If camouflaged with your own
voice and the individual is not interlocked with discernment,
well, it could open a gateway of immeasurable proportions
of extirpation for your life; this is Satan's primary objective.
Relatively, a person who serves the Lord or not, doesn't have
this kind of understanding to distinguish certain pernicious
thinking, consequently following and speaking whatever
enters their heart and allocating whatever flows out of their

mouth which we call blurting, offensive, and disrespectful speech becomes dangerous if he doesn't have a close relationship with Christ to know the difference.
Out of the abundance of the heart the mouth will speak.

*A good man out of the good treasure of his heart brings forth good; and an evil man out of the evil treasure of his heart brings forth evil. For* **out of the abundance of the heart his mouth speaks**.
**Luke 6:45** *(NKJV)* Emphasis added.

*For as he thinks in his heart, so is he.*
**Prov. 23:7** *(NKJV)*

## NO RESPECT

There has been a magnitude of people around the world knowing first hand what I am writing about. Satan is making sure we stay in a cloud of lustful cravings of endless satisfaction to bring us a zenith of disease and false dominance. Society and the world are always pushing lust persistently to be related to sex, but not always Saints, in fact, it's also associated with greed for power and control as you have read, but the general public tells us otherwise. This is a Jezebel spirit in its purest form by the influence of Belial a demon general of Satan's kingdom as I pointed out earlier. A relationship with worldliness and distorted views falls into the lap of fools on such a greater intensity level. Belial and Jezebel are interrelated, we cannot take part at all with darkness, but many are yoked in spiritual slavery and don't even know it. Unequivocally, we know better, we are supposed to be a light in a dark place, and salt in a world that has lost its flavor. In our day, unsaved people can't tell the world from a Christian, because we all look and sound alike. An epicenter of distinct change has to be the attribute of all people of God, so we could come out from among them and be separate.

I concur to a certain degree we must become all things to all people to win some, that's very true. Although, to stride on another level, we must do this with the <u>leading</u> of the Holy Spirit adhering to His counsel at all times from the Spirit, not from your theological degrees and head knowledge of the Word. As a peculiar people and a holy nation, keep in mind Satan does not respect the Bible, esteem holy reverence, or worships God, like some Muslims believe. Why? For the simple fact he knows the Bible better than you do! Satan does not respect paper and ink. When you read the Word of God, it means nothing but words on a page; therefore, respect will not suffice in his eyes. The devil respects and gives reverence to the Holy Spirit! Now, combine the believer with the paper and ink enthralled together with the Spirit of Christ who is in you the hope of all Glory, BAAM!!! Satan submits to your authority, until then, you must watch and pray and keep yourself from idols. Idols can be anything you love more than God. (1) Children (2) Spouse (3) House (4) Car (5) Lust (6) Pornography (7) Yourself. Now, painting this picture for you is why we can't *always* become all things to all people because then it would leave room for error and confusion. The believer must be careful at all times and not enter a situation with out the Spirit of God ahead of you and meeting you there. You have to walk in, walk with, and walk by, the power of Christ's Spirit. There is no other way.

*Do not be unequally yoked together with unbelievers. For what fellowship has righteousness with lawlessness? And what communion has light with darkness? And **what accord has Christ with Belial**? Or what part has a believer with an unbeliever?*
***2 Cor. 6:14-15*** *(NKJV)* Emphasis added.

*Certain men,* **the children of Belial***, are gone out from among you, and have withdrawn the inhabitants of their city, saying, Let us go and serve other gods, which ye have not known; Then shalt thou enquire, and make search, and ask diligently; and, behold, if it be truth, and the thing certain, that such abomination is wrought among you; Thou shalt surely smite the inhabitants of that city with the edge of the sword, destroying it utterly, and all that is therein, and the cattle thereof, with the edge of the sword.*
**Deut. 13:13-15** *(KJV)* Emphasis added.


## PROTECT THE SHEEP FROM FALSE DESIRES

Some pastors and ministers can tell the voice of the devil in a second with no hesitation, seeing that it is insidious and hurtful to their flock, they will war and pray against that spirit to bring liberation. Since love and awareness rests on the mantle of their hearts, they also know first hand, if some of their congregants have heard the real voice of our adversary, or they manifest from the spirit realm and physically touch the believer, fear will begin to surmount and deliverance must take place. Therefore, needing either the pastor, apostle, or minister to facilitate and assist with the purpose of overcoming any confusion and bring understanding to that situation. I have a trained ear to know the distinction of the voice of God and the voice of the devil. Brother, sister, hear me good. You must know how to attune the voices to know if it's you, God, or the devil. There are many voices out in our world today, mostly is to bring turmoil and tragedy, others redemption and beauty for ashes.

**My sheep hear My voice***, and I know them, and they follow Me.*
**John 10:27** *(NKJV)* Emphasis added.

*And when he putteth forth his own sheep, he goeth before them, and the sheep follow him: for they know his voice. And a stranger will they not follow, but will flee from him: for they know not the voice of strangers.*
**John 10:4-5** *(KJV)*

## PRAYER FOR GUIDANCE

Father, I pray that you will help me know the difference between You and the voices of the enemy, whether through people or from the supernatural. Help me to stay away from all types of fleshly lusts, and evil desires of greed, wants, control which is rebellion and witchcraft which can cause me to fall away from you. Holy Spirit I ask you in the name of Jesus, show me if there is anything in me that is not like you to come into being so I could repent and move forward. I thank you God that you have given me the authority to cast down wicked imaginations and the enabling to rebuke demonic activity of all sorts. I praise your name for the goodness and mercy you have shown me, that I may never take it for granted. I receive the guiding of the Holy Ghost to empower me like never before in the matchless name of Jesus Christ. Amen.

# PURPOSE DRIVEN WORSHIP

# Chapter Eight

PURPOSE
    DRIVEN
        WORSHIP

*Finally, brethren, whatever things are true, whatever things are noble, whatever things are just, whatever things are pure, whatever things are lovely, whatever things are of good report, if there is any virtue and if there is anything praiseworthy–meditate on these things. The things, which you learned and received and heard and saw in me, these do, and the God of peace will be with you.*

**—Philippians 4:8-9**

A GUIDEBOOK HAS BEEN WRITTEN before you were ever born or thought of, to help unlock your true purpose. Your inheritance has already been established since the foundation of the world, you just have to walk into it. The awesome thing about it, God has made a way and made a *promise plan* for your life before creation came into fruition. You are unique in your own way. Never think less of yourself no matter the condition you're in. You were the only one on His mind when you were created in your mother's womb, a one on one appointment. Since you are reading this, it proves that you want to know who you are and why you're here. Prepare yourself to explore your architectural blueprint to build a foundation of stability and ascend with purpose, so the amazing plan of God that has been set before you would flourish. Moreover, destiny is written all over the DNA of your spirit.

Placed
Under His
Rest &
Purpose
Offering
Salvation for
Everyone

## YOUR REASON FOR LIVING

Now that you know the "Lambs Book of Life" has your name written therein, it is time to dive into the pool of purpose. Worship is already within you, whether you sense it or not, it is. Even when you don't feel anointed, you are. Just when you think He left, He hasn't. Realizing that the Messiah has come to give us a reason to live life to the fullest, and in complete abundance is an awe-inspiring idea. Recognizing your purpose and potential with full conviction and certainty, is just the outer ring of something fresh and new ready to commence in your time. Praise must flow through your veins with the ability to adore His move in the spirit. Worshipping God is a power that has been given to you, to divide and conquer the enemy's ruse coming against you, and those you are hoping for to come to Christ. According to what the Word says, if we do not have any *hope* it makes a heart of a person sick afflicting them to give up on life as a whole, this is when wholeness comes in. You have much to offer to the Body of Christ and the world, I encourage you not to give up...Keep on walking with fervor and a fire for God, and you will see a change in your attitude and in the same token, spill into your ill situations.

*Hope deferred makes the heart sick, but when the desire comes, it is a tree of life.*
**Prov. 13:12** *(NKJV)*

## MIND GAMES

The devil will always paint a picture of you, in your own mind, making you sense you are unimportant and that everyone you encounter detest you. He will push you to feel ostracized, so when your friends and family come around you, it will seem that no one enjoys your company. He will play mind games, discouraging your hope and faith to the point of giving up on everything. The goal of Satan is very clear, as you continue living life, you will see he never uses new tactics. Like a game of chess, demonic intervention will downpour into your life qualifying you as a weak target. Where is his playing field? Your mind is his playing field, thus, when you hear the words, "You're out!" it is what it is. He longs to make sure you do not know who you are, so the fruit of Christ will not come to pass. His objective is to grab hold of your desire for righteousness, kill it, and smash it, until there is none left, and the end result; for you to lose the will to go on. The wicked one knows if you allow yourself to keep moving ahead and not turn back to your old sinful ways, he can prevent your spiritual tree from blossoming. The kingdom of Satan, and his evil horde, wishes for you to stay in darkness, knowing if you come to the light, you will begin to produce good fruit in abundance custom designed for yourself, to be a blessing toward others.

*Even so, every good tree bears good fruit, but a bad tree bears bad fruit. A good tree cannot bear bad fruit, nor can a bad tree bear good fruit. Every tree that does not bear good fruit is cut down and thrown into the fire. Therefore by their fruits you will know them.*
**Matt. 7:17-20** *(NKJV)*

*For a good tree does not bear bad fruit, nor does a bad tree bear good fruit. For every tree is known by its own fruit. For men do not gather figs from thorns, nor do they gather grapes from a bramble bush.*
**Luke 6:43-44** *(NKJV)*

## PURPOSE DRIVEN WORSHIP

Make it brighter wherever you are, exhibiting a true paradigm of being a man or woman of righteousness, perseverance, and an example for others. Adulation toward God is a privilege beyond wonders, miracles, and human imagination–in the same instance He inhabits your praises. His presence is worth more than a thousand universes. His voice is "Still," and the "Calm," which follows after, burns on the inside of you as a wild fire with the fragrance suffering the room with the breath of His presence. The firm vocals of rushing water–resonates out of Him exploding you into a different dimension of purpose and power unknown to the world we live in. You must come to the realization that true worship, is when you are behind closed doors at home when no one is watching.

Every time your heart beats you could feel His heart beat at the same time. When He whispers in your ear to instruct you, you can sense His breathing on your face. A sweet aroma of His love and majesty will surround you, until you are consumed with His presence. We must learn again to serenade Him and place everyone on hold, as we should. Living for Him with our voice, living for Him with our hands, living for Him with our feet, blesses His heart in the highest status. Worshipping Him with every ounce and fiber of your being you were created to be, is saying you really love the fact that He exists for you alone. A personal Lord and Savior who is there for you thanking Him always, for saving your life from the ill wills of society, shattering the hands of the devil off you. When God exhales, it sparks and ignites the anointing residing in your spirit, enabling you to love others and the Lord, with gladness and meekness in total submission. Sometimes we have to be still enough for us to accede the Holy Ghost with our total being. Honesty and sincerity must cascade onto those around you, especially those in the faith. Covering you with His wings of healing, and overcoming you with His shadow, will definitely be an advantage over the enemy, fulfilling your true purpose in your everyday life. His grace will overflow and His face will shine through you in the Light, which will pierce any darkness with eternal power and confidence. When the Holy Spirit begins to do that, you have walked into the front door of your true purpose in Christ, with assurance this will amplify purpose driven worship.

Now it is time to push ahead into the promises of God that have been promised to you.

*He who dwells in the secret place of the Most High Shall* ***abide under the shadow*** *of the Almighty. I will say of the LORD, "He is my refuge and my fortress; My God, in Him I will trust." Surely He shall deliver you from the snare of the fowler and from the perilous pestilence.*
***Psalms 91:1-3*** *(NKJV)* Emphasis added.

*For* ***all the promises*** *of God in Him are Yes, and in Him Amen, to the glory of God through us.*
***2 Cor. 1:20*** *(NKJV)*

## COMPASSION TOWARD GOD

God is very compassionate and merciful. We must come to a point of truly becoming what He desires for us to be. Worship helps you become one with God. Bringing it back to where it should've been. Vast amounts of people have forgotten how it used to be when the Spirit of the Lord would arrive and move in the earth. He would ride the wind with His voice, which He did once before in the *cool of the day*. When this occurs healing takes place, many would be made whole, blinded eyes would see, and the deaf ears would open. Allowing God to radiate in the center of your soul, teaching you His ways will permit you to prevail over your stresses and perplexities. Let His will reign in you for the remainder of your days. His compassion and mercy will overwhelm your storms without the slightest effort on His part, if you give in to Him. If you have a burdensome load to carry, do not stray from Him when His hands are reaching down to you. He holds everything together by the Word of His power. Revere the Lord, and give Him praise knowing He deserves it for the kindness He has shown you. A God that is, exemplifies a character of love, admiration, and a willingness to bring you up when you are down trodden. Compassion, defines showing compassion or being merciful. Are we as compassionate as we ought to be? The Rock of Ages has said time and time again, that He is the very source of your strength, when you feel exhausted from trying to overcome daily battles in your mind. We must go back and reduce ourselves in His presence and influence, to enable us to counter attack the enemy with potency.

His tender mercies and great forgiveness will consistently restore you, as His compassion takes residence in your circumstance. Hence, you have to repurify the embrace of oneness again to the Lord, for the simple truth He is always in a position to receive your adoration. Believers tend to react to God's love, with selfish actions and wicked ambitions. Jesus always tried to get the Pharisees and Sadducees to see clearly, He desired obedience above sacrifice, and not the facade of one's religious position. Adonai is never in a specific mood one day and then changes the next day, as if He were bi-polar. He is always in a place of having open arms, outstretched, to make sure that you know He will always be there for you. On the basis of understanding Him fully, He will have you maneuver in ways that can bring confusion, not saying He is confused or brings confusion since He is not the author of it, but with the understanding that He never shows you the big picture all at once. You cannot figure God out, giving in and leaning on His ways shows the Lord we are submissive, obedient, and patient enough to wait on Him. Knowing your true purpose in your life and being aware of various types of ways the enemy tries to slip in will be simple to distinguish, if you submit to Christ wholeheartedly.

Letting your eyes wonder in a distant gaze enamored with different spirits and their impious movements and softness of touch, will slowly arrest you in a cave of darkness and shame. God must reign always in your heart and mind or the blessings will not come down from the Father of Lights. Let your life emanate His Wisdom, who is The Messiah, guiding and embracing you at all times with the warmth of His precious Spirit. He is our salvation our strength and deliverer. When we really need Him, He will always show up. His healing rain will fall on us once again to make us strong even when we do not deserve it. The entire world is going to experience and literally see, that Jesus is alive and well, in the very near future. Chains will be broken; lives will be healed in every area, as long as we walk after His Spirit on a consistent everyday basis, for tomorrow is not promised to anyone.

*But God, who is rich in mercy, because of His great love with which He loved us, even when we were dead in trespasses, made us alive together with Christ (by grace you have been saved), and raised us up together, and made us sit together in the heavenly places in Christ Jesus, that in the ages to come He might show the exceeding riches of His grace in His kindness toward us in Christ Jesus. For by grace you have been saved through faith, and that not of yourselves; it is the gift of God, not of works, lest anyone should boast.*
**Eph. 2:4-9** *(NKJV)*

## A.S.K. GOD

**A**sk. **S**eek. **K**nock.

His truth will make us free, indeed, always and forever. Ask God for His holy kiss; ask God, how are you feeling today? Ask God, what can I do for you today, Lord? We're always asking Him to do things for us, why not ask God, Daddy, what would you like me to do for you today? Or, What would you like me to do for someone else to be a blessing? Spend time with your heavenly Father.

## OVERPOWERED BY LOVE

Let His Hallelujah explode inside your members like a wild fire. Let the blaze of His Son's power inflict us with goodness. Let it burn in the depths of our bones, shut up in your members. Let God reign in your soul. His pillar cloud of fire in the Spirit will lead and over take you, guiding you into a new day of restoration and peace. Let the grown men fall onto their knees again, hugging themselves in the sight of God, individually declaring, how much He misses His Creator from his youth and how much he adores and loves Him. Especially, allowing the Holy Spirit to become your hiding place and total fulfillment in your outer end. Draw closer as a broken vessel, and He can flow and fill you spiritually, until you are old and feeble, ready to enter into the arms of Eternity. The Lord will make Himself strong in your weaknesses. At this level you will be able to make an impact in the life of a sister or brother, who are struggling and being hit with all diverse kinds of situations. Let His truth raise you into an adult of integrity, subsequently you will be able to find yourself. Let his grace be greater than your whispers of condemnation of your own heart. Born again into a new image, the image of Christ, the Wonderful who sits High and looks low (Isaiah

9:6). Allow the Counselor to counsel your mind smitten with total transformation. Put your life in His hand. Let Him walk up and down in the midst of your heart, so when the Great Physician opens you up, He can see His Son's footprints of hosanna and mercy, has stepped into a new place, containing a heartbeat of holy love with His Son's imagery on the surface of your own spirit.

God is a veil of righteousness hovering in front of your vision, and when He speaks to you, the veil is removed to clearly see His Holiness and Majesty. Cherubim's and His Seraphim's yell with a high-powered voice saying aloud how majestic Adonai really is. When they see the veil removed from the eyes of humans, the heavens rejoice and a warm chill falls from the top of your head down to the depth of your being. Feeling His presence with flames of fire from His eyes overcomes you to the full. His love is burning the heart of souls and the ears of His people causing them to return to Him, always preparing a place of new heights and healing for all men. Open your eyes to His wonders and worship. He fills you from on High causing everyone to become jealous of you. We look just like Him. We are an exact image in His Son. The Holy Spirit extends His glory and exhortations to the inner man, we must let Him do this. Always position yourself to the epicenter of truth and edification, honoring His commandments on the highest level of anointing. Purity through worship is showing Him that you are available at all times, to your God who **is** love. He doesn't have love He is love. Humble yourself before His Holy Mountain. Let the prophet humble himself, let the pastor fall to his knees, let the evangelist speak softly. Let every nation be still, and fall prostrate in adoration in the company of our Majesty. This is a small scenario of what it is to be on familiar terms in purpose driven worship in your life and for your life…a result of spiritual enrichment, by worshipping God with all your existence.

# LIVE LONG AND MAKE A DIFFERENCE

As we get older we are suppose to get wiser in our lives knowing we don't have long to live on earth, desiring our years to mean something when its time to move on to the next world. God never said that we would live seventy years and if by strength eighty. That was a prayer of Moses to God on the behalf of his dealings with the Lord and toward the children of Israel in Psalms 90:10. God mentioned man's lifespan in Genesis chapter 6:3, stating that mankind will live up to one hundred and twenty years of age, this is the last time God declared how long man would live. Mainly, proving to humans the reason for people all around the world who are reaching the age of one hundred and eighteen, which is no surprise to the believer who knows what the Living Letter declares. No one in all of history since He said that Word in the Book of Genesis, lived more than one hundred and twenty years for it would violate Genesis 6, plus God will ever let that happen. Personally, I believe Christians pass on, and sinners pass away, nonetheless, God's heart of compassion, mercy, love, and faithfulness is such a small part of who He totally is as our Master and Lord. He will make sure we are absent from this body and present with Him forever! This is why worshipping Him in spirit and with pure truth is so important. Having a heart of purpose driven worship is so inspiring, it will move in the hearts and minds of the most vile of all creation. Lets worship and praise God the way King David did, when he asked the Lord to give him a clean heart. This is beyond dancing in the spirit, ask Him how to do it, I guarantee you He will perform His Word in and around you, if you ask with a clean and pure heart.

## PRAYER OF WORSHIP AND PRAISE

Ancient of Days you are my oxygen when it becomes difficult to breathe. Be my strength from within my inner man when I am weak. You are my divan I rest on when the sheets over come me. You are my wind when the fire gets too hot. You are my hands when I can't no longer hold on. You are my feet when I can't move forward to bring good news because I am flooded with evil all around me. Lord you are my eyes when I am sleeping, watching over me, to make sure the enemy doesn't injure me. I worship you father always and forever. Amazed and in awe of your presence is my establishment. The songs I sing, the tears I cry, and the yells I scream are never on deaf ears. Oh, Father, how your love reigns within me. How you never forgotten me when my spouse left me. How you never condemn me when I fell away and came back for the reason your love and mercy was so influential and overpowering, surrender was the only absolution. Thank you Father, for your endless and irresistible Love. In the name of Jesus. Amen.

# CHAPTER NINE

# THE LIVING WATER

# Chapter Nine

## THE LIVING
## WATER

*As Scripture says, 'Streams of living water will flow*
*from deep within the person who believes in me'.*

**—John 7:38**

THERE IS A BIG DIFFERENCE BETWEEN sinners and saints as you examine them both. Sinners practice sin, saints practice righteousness. When a pianist practices on his piano and hits the wrong note he doesn't continue hitting the wrong note, he goes back and corrects it and tries not to hit that key again. Therefore, he is practicing how to hit all the right things in order for perfection and success to visit him in the future. A sinner does not. A sinner wallows and practices sin, everyday. He doesn't repent or feel bad when he sins against himself or someone else. No, he looks forward to do it again with no conviction in his spirit, especially if his conscience is seared with a hot iron, like numerous believers. He doesn't have the Holy Spirit correcting him, like saints do before they do or say something wrong. Basically, he is doing what he is supposed to be doing as a child of the enemy. Again, the right thought voice comes into your mind first, as I expressed earlier, as the second one comes to deceive you to fall into a trap of despair. Which one will you follow? Most assuredly, many of us follow after the louder voice. My focal point is the Christian has to come to an apex, allowing the Holy Ghost to arrest his spirit and take him captive. Apostle Paul said it best asserting that he is a prisoner of the Lord Jesus Christ, sanctioning himself to be captured by The Master (Ephesians 3:1 & Colossians 4:3).

This is to fundamentally understand who the *Living Water* is. I have to reiterate this again because it is so important to the Christian regarding the sacrifice that was provided for all humans to receive as a free gift which in turn cost Christ everything. When you illustrate contumacy against Christ you are telling God that the ultimate sacrifice he stipulated is meager and inconsequential. God gets offended when a human being rejects His idea of sacrificing His only born Son. We are plainly spitting in His face saying, "What you did for me was hollow and vain." Think about that for a moment. It is dreadful to even write or talk about, especially to the sinner and the backslider when it comes to the offering of His only Son. Please be aware of the high cost the Lord had to endure. Placing this under the list of things that are vanity in your head will never come to means for what God has done for all humanity. Turn and change for the better and submit to His will as you give up yours. Why? Because we ALL were bought at a high price, our lives are not our own! Assuredly, many don't turn to the Messiah, finding they are angry with God or mad with people who have hurt them in the past. Remember the past is inside of you. So when people say leave things in the past, how could you, if the past dwells within yourself? This means you need to be free from something greater than you, and Christ Jesus can liberate you instantly and sometimes with others gradually. In the same case He will do it no matter the wait, but will you allow patience to have its work in you to be like Jesus? If someone has hurt you, or you are walking around at home, work, church, or any other place you can think of, being angry, God wants to heal you right where you are hurting.

## THE SPIRIT OF ANGER

Anger is a very strong spirit. Therapists believe anger is a very strong emotion. Although, both are correct there is a lesson to be learned here. I for one have dealt with anger on a great level. It caused me to be very bitter and unforgiving toward anyone who caused me to get upset or has offended me. Anger is a very brawny spirit. I used to feel the rise inside of the center of my belly and would give full vent to it, and being familiar with the Book of Proverbs, I became a fool. There is a difference when you have fits of rage and furious anger. It did not matter to me who you were; I would just blow up without a lot happening around me. Alas, my family had dealt with this for a very long time. This fierceness will take a toll on your heart and mind. You will start to think about things you never would think of in a bad situation. The greater the hurt, the greater the pain you want to inflict on the other person. Radical demonic thoughts of fury would pound on your mind like if you were a volcano; waiting for just one more word or situation to come about, and you are ready to explode! Just like God gets glory when we praise and honor Him, Satan also gets his glory, praise and honor, but with evil doing.

*Make no friendship with an angry man, and with a furious man do not go, lest you learn his ways and set a snare for your soul.*
**Prov. 22:24-25** *(NKJV)*

*A fool expresses all his emotions, but a wise person controls them.*
**Prov. 29:11** *(Gods Word)*

*Be angry, and do not sin. Meditate within your heart on your bed, and be still.*
**Psalms 4:4** *(NKJV)*

*Be angry, and do not sin...*
**Eph. 4:26** (NKJV)


Anger for me is now an emotion, when before it was a spirit. You have to catch it Saints, it is very critical that you do. Believe me, anger is not an emotion to play with, it is a very serious 'feeling'. There were times the anger was so bad I couldn't even keep my head together. I thank God that I get angry in my head and not within my belly, which I used to feel deep down, rising on the inside, exploding me into an unknown person. It was terrible when that would happen. Then control began to form, and all different pathways that I didn't want to walk through, but I did anyway. I had to learn to forgive and forget just like Jesus did for me. Forgetting was the part that became the hardest if you do not stay under the blood of reconciliation. I really did not want to forgive my enemies, my family, and friends for what they did to me. And the Lord intervened and said, "Son, you have done things to others that you have forgotten, remember I have already forgiven you for your sins against Me, so you are going to forgive others." When He spoke to me about forgiveness and letting go of the junk within myself, at first I rebelled, but as time went by I yielded to His will so I could be made free. Partaking from the Living Water and walking in a persuaded mindset, will always bring deliverance to those who run with fortitude for change in their lives. I advise anyone who deals with anger to go before the Holy Counselor and seek His guidance. I am living proof that He will set and make you free!

*Do not hasten in your spirit to be angry, for anger rests in the bosom of fools.*
**Eccl. 7:9** *(NKJV)*

*Remember this, my dear brothers and sisters: Everyone…should not get angry easily.*
**James 1:19** *(Gods Word)*


## SIMILAR EXPERIENCE

Heaven is a real place. Hell is a real place. God doesn't send anyone to hell. You send yourself there by rejecting Christ (Rom. 6:23, 1 Jn. 5:12, Rom. 3:23). To the theologian, I understand that God does send you there Himself because of the power that He contains to send you. I am writing from a spiritual aspect with basic teaching for all believers corporately. Beside the 2,084 most talked about verses in observing money in the Bible, hell came in second place. Why? His desire for you is not to go there. It's a terrible place. A friend of mine in the past had a girlfriend who was visited by Jesus. Jesus would take her to hell in a span of three days to experience what its like down there, and then she would come back to her own body. She told her boyfriend to help her understand why the Lord will allow this. Every time she came back to earth she would ask him to prepare ice baths in the morning, so when she returns, she could cool off. She explained to me the ice felt like a semi-hot bath water. She kept telling me, even though her body wasn't burning physically, it was her soul underneath her flesh that was feeling the pain of the extreme heat. I listened intensely as she went on, believing her story since there are many books and living witnesses who have gone through similar experiences. Additionally, I had my own experiences seeing the demonic and angelic realm. I was able to understand the out of body occurrences she had gone through. I recall, when I saw the angels of God, the Lord allowed the light realm to slow down for me, to get a glimpse of the supernatural and how it operates. Natural light is really slow compared to the angels of God and God Himself who is the Father of all Lights. Revealing that His angels could travel around the globe seven and a half times in one second and return to the same spot they left prior—now that's fast! Our children have also seen angels standing in their room with a shield, a sword in hand, and clothes, which were part of their skin, but yet transparent. I seen thousands of them as dazzling bright white lights and others were totally different, with the appearance of what I would describe as celestial firelights, but these traveled at a slower speed.

*Every good gift and every perfect gift is from above, and comes down from the* **Father of lights**, *with whom there is no variation or shadow of turning.* **James 1:17** *(NKJV)* Emphasis added.


## WHICH SIDE ARE YOU ON?

This is not a place of waiting until you are good enough; this is a real tangible place. Proverbs 8:36 say, "All who hate me, love death." In the same reference, the Holy Spirit is not a God we can push to the side when things get out of hand. Somehow we must come to terms and meet the Lord where He is. Communication has always been the key with God. Conformity to be a living sacrifice is in the limelight, along with all that the Lord has for us if we follow His examples. Sanctity must be the main objective to every Christian, to ensure holiness. The Lord uttered, "Without holiness no one will see Him." If you find yourself in a situation that is very hard to break out of, immediately get in contact with your apostle, bishop, or pastor, someone who will help you through your struggles, and walks in power, holiness, and strong deliverance. Staying in a situation that would lead anyone to a place of eternal misery, and destruction, is not worth losing your soul over. Take into account the story of the rich man, *Mr. Divies* in Luke chapter 16. (*The Rich man, Mr. Divies and Lazarus; not to confuse the Lazarus whom was raised from death after four days*). Lazarus would beg at the home of the rich man, with the expectancy of crumbs falling from the rich man's table so he can eat. I can relate with Lazarus. (I had my share of homelessness similar to Lazarus, begging people to have something to eat, wearing the same clothes everyday and then afterwards, wondering when will I eat again). At that time, that was my hell. Immeasurably, of course, this experience with the rich man being in hell is considered to be beyond human calculation, compared to my homelessness.

Jesus distinctively revealed a spiritual secret of the unknown to us (Deut. 29:29, Daniel 2:28, Isaiah 45:3). Now we know without a shadow of a doubt that hell exists. The proper term in the New Testament is hades. Hades is not hell; Gehenna, which is mentioned four times in the Bible, is literally translated as "Hell." This is just theologically being correct. For the sake of simplicity we will go with hades being hell, which is sort of similar, the reason being is because both places are hot, and easier to understand without all the breakdowns of derivatives and languages. The Gospel of Luke chapter 16:23, Mr. Divies lifted his eyes and saw Abraham and Lazarus afar off, enjoying the eternal comfort of God's paradise. A great 'Chasm' meaning, a deep opening, like an abyss in the earth, separated them one from another. To his amazement the rich man, *Mr. Divies*, starts yelling out to father Abraham to give him water to cool his tongue because of the torment of fire, and eternal anguish he is suffering. This story is incredible, mysterious, and frightening; the Lord's heart is not for anyone to go there. Nevertheless, millions everyday choose that path by whirling away the plan of redemption. Dolefully, according to statistics, one hundred and fifty million people are born every year, and out of that number, only one hundred and fifty thousand give their lives to Christ, that's about ten percent, while the rest remain lost. We must bring up those numbers quickly—Where are the evangelists? We need to work fast, all of us. Please, lets go out to the ghettos, suburbs, inner cities, everywhere, and lets go get them! So where we are, they can be also!

The world today and the Christian claim that America is a Christian nation, I say we are not a Christian nation, we used to be; now we are a nation with Christians in it. We as a nation of Christians must come together so we can have an encounter with the Living Water on a more unequivocal vast scale; to refresh us who are already saved and also be able to lead more souls into heaven so others can believe the reality that Christ exists Proverbs 11:30, Daniel 12:3, and James 5:20. Virtually, sinners claim to believe and they do right by believing in God, however, so does the devil. What's it going to take for that sinner to repent before death knocks on the door of his heart? The answer is nothing, until he realizes he needs a Savior for his soul to be redeemed. Again, sinners believe, and so does the devil, but Saints confess one to another, to bring hope and healing.

## GOD WILL NEVER DO THAT, OR WILL HE?

We are blessed that He has chosen us to bear His fruit and establish His Word throughout the entire planet (John 15:16). The Lord revealed to me that He wouldn't save everyone, not to misconstrue that He can save, but in the arena that its up to the individual to say 'Yes' to His Son, Jesus, in order to be saved (I am fully aware of Calvinism, which is not the view here). It's true when you meditate on the fact its up to us to make the ultimate decision to be saved. The misconception on a broader scale will bring you to a crossroad that Christ will not save everyone because it's all predestined in His mind, He knows who will make it or not. In a similar affair, God needs someone who will reject Him to use that person to glorify the Lord as in the days with Pharaoh, and countless others. He did say He would have mercy, and compassion on whom He wishes, a vessel for destruction and another for honor (See Romans 9:1-23). If the Lord saved everyone, then who are these people Jesus is going to destroy at the end of the seven-year tribulation? The Messiah is going to take vengeance on humans, those who rejected Him and lived a life of sin and rebellion. I know this might sound harsh but it's in the Word.

Sorry to say, there is copious amount of Christians ignorant to what the Bible proclaims about a lot of different subjects. Plus, Jesus did say, "Revenge is mine, I shall repay." On whom is He taking out His revenge? Sinners! Why would there be a White Throne Judgment, if every single person were saved? Its up to the person to make that final decision before the curtain comes down and the show is over. This is evidence that there will be many loved ones, or people we had known and not known on earth, who decided to go the other way, turned the other cheek and didn't make it to heaven with us. I believe, the reason multitudes of Christians do not believe in a God that will do such things is the fact they never read the back of the Book called 'Revelation', and pastors don't teach this book in Sunday school or the podium as they should. I have studied and still study the Book of Revelation since 1987 and the scrolls, seals, and bowls of judgment are still the same today, as they were thousands of years ago, as foretold by the major prophets of the Old Testament. Every time I speak to a non-believer, or a backslidden Christian, they constantly give me the excuse that they are busy. They are busy doing this, busy doing that, busy going here, and busy going there, especially on Sunday. All these justifiable reasons to avoid visiting the house of God. I heard it so much there is an acronym for it.

**B**.eing **U**.nder **S**.atans **Y**.oke. They might as well profess this to be a fact with all the defenses and excuses they use.

## HARD TO HEAR

I know this might be tough to comprehend and take in, and it's a horrible thought to process. Periodically, we have to realize that God is not just a God of love, but He is also a God of judgment and justice in the same sentence. As I mentioned in the earlier chapters we need to stop placing the Lord in a box. He can destroy a person if He wanted too, and create another one just like him. Not saying that God will do that, knowing full well He desires for many to go to heaven, but it saddens His heart seeing sinners and backsliders by the millions every year going into hell. (In the Psalms it declares that hell is never full it always want more and more). We must take into account, not to take advantage of Father God and His mercy and grace; He is not a figurine to play with. On the other side of the fence, thousands would reject the love of the Son of Lights (1 John 5:11, 12). We do not know who has chosen God according to their motive and intellect, therefore, making an empathetic decision within themselves; but it does create an opportunity for us to have a fervent attitude to push forth, and diligently work to preach and teach the Gospel of Christ with fervor to every creature, not knowing with complete assurance who is going to heaven or not. I don't have a heaven or hell to give to anyone; our responsibility is to make sure we get as many as we can into the kingdom where Christ resides. So we must teach anyone who has an ear to hear and letting Adonai make that final verdict. Until then, our lost family members need our prayers everyday so the Lord can intervene on our behalf to dodge the possibility of our loved ones being placed in the center of hell's torment. Everyday I ask God to save my two younger brothers, just like the rich man in the New Testament. As you read Luke 16, the rich man had five other brothers he begged not to be where he is. He kept pleading with father Abraham to get him out of that anguish and torture of fire burning him all over his body and in the inner and outer parts of his soul, with a worm that crawls and slithers in, around, and over him and all those who go there.

*...Where their worm does not die, and the fire is not quenched.*
**Mark 9:48** *(NKJV)*

I entreat all those who confess Christ from their lips, but their hearts are far away from Him, to evade from becoming a fallen soul that would never again remember the great memories of his family, friends and this life, but constant torment of, "I should've changed and listened when they told me about accepting Jesus and now its too late for me." All those who go to hell will never hear the sound of birds chirping or seeing a beautiful sunset again. In hell, there are snakes of all sizes, spiders, pain, gnarling, regret, resentment, screaming, fire, torment, and eternal suffering. Also a darkness that could be felt just like it was in the days of Pharaoh, illustrated perfectly according to the Old Testament in the Book of Exodus. (This experience was very similar to mine as you read chapter ten).

*Then the* LORD *said to Moses, "Stretch out your hand toward heaven, that there may be darkness over the land of Egypt, darkness which may even be felt."*
**Ex. 10:21** *(NKJV)*

To bring back to your recollection, the Holy Ghost dwells and takes residence deep down in the inner most part of your spirit. With that in mind, Christians who are in right standing with God, and those who are not really taking into deliberation that these are not just stories that Jesus made up. The born again believer must avoid at all costs going back to their old life again. Demonic spirits can't wait to enter into a backslider and possess their body. Be possessed by the Holy Spirit, the Living Water. He is joy unspeakable! He is the Spirit of power, love and a sound mind in every born from above Christian believer.

*...Do not sorrow, for the joy of the LORD is your strength.*
**Neh. 8:10** *(NKJV)*

*For God has not given us a spirit of fear, but of power and of love and of a sound mind.*
**2 Tim. 1:7** *(NKJV)*

Although, these verses are written in the Bible from the Lord Himself with the hand of man, there is that specific individual who just will not believe, regardless of the truth that has been spoken. However, the final truth is, there are no unbelievers when death comes to receive them. The final certainty is they're not able to come back and tell us that the next world either heaven or hell actually does exist.

Occasionally, you would have a particular group, selected by God, who had passed over into the realm of the spirit and then experiencing hell first hand, and finally returning to inform us of what they've seen. It was a blessing for me that I didn't have to stay in a dead state in order to see Satan for myself, knowing the silver cord was not cut from my body from my soul and spirit. What do I mean? According to Scripture and my occurrence, there is a silver cord that is attached to you when you have an out of body experience, or actual physical death when the Lord takes you to hell or heaven. Let me remind you 'death' is not the cessation of our lives. Death in the Holy Scriptures is always pointed of being separated from your earth shell, called the body. Essentially, you will go back into your flesh–your body, until the Lord allows that 'silver cord' to be cut. When it does get cut, the person is permanently deceased.

*Remember your Creator before the **silver cord** is loosed, or the golden bowl is broken, or the pitcher shattered at the fountain, or the wheel broken at the well. Then the **dust** [man] **will return to the earth** as it was, and **the spirit** [man] **will return to God** who gave it.*
**Eccl. 12:6-7** *(NKJV)*. Emphasis added.

## THE MESSIAH ON HIS THRONE

Reading the passages about the Lord resting His feet on the earth as His footstool really came alive for me in 2003. "Whether in the body or out of the body I am not certain, but I know this, immediately I was caught up in the spirit and I saw Him sitting on His Throne in heaven! He was Glorious! Sitting high and looking low! His hair was a medium brown, and you could see through His body, leaning towards transparency but at the same time, He was there in flesh and bone as the Scriptures proclaim, but glorified.

*Behold My hands and My feet, that it is I Myself* [Jesus]. *Handle Me and see, for a spirit does not have **flesh and bones** as you see I have.*
**Luke 24:39** *(NKJV)* Emphasis added.

It's really difficult to explain what His skin and body looked like. He had a Golden Crown on His head, and inside of His crown were millions of the same golden crown within. Immediately I thought, "WOW! This *is* the KING of KINGS!" "PRAISE GOD IN THE HIGHEST!" *(Jesus is Beautiful and Magnificent)*. The best I can describe it is, His clothes were part of His skin, and also the archangel standing near Him, whom I believe was Michael. He was at attention ready to fight if he was commanded to implement war! The Archangel was taller than the earth, maybe about 50,000 miles tall. The Iron Scepter that was in Jesus' right hand was elevated slowly and then–Wham! He slammed it down quickly against the southern part of the universe and into the southern part of the earth, with tremendous power! It sounded like a thunder crack, times a billion! It was sonorous! And yet, not deafening to my ear. As He stood up, He said in a stentorian voice, JUDGMENT!!! I knew right then, this judgment was after the seventh year of The Tribulation period known as the Second Coming of God's Messiah. The Lord showed me the future of all the wicked, the countries which were destroyed since the children of disobedience discarded the fact of taking the Holy path of righteousness and repentance. They also abandoned the sacrifice of His Son and His Word by their disobedient conduct.

**The scepter** *shall not depart from Judah, Nor a lawgiver from between his feet, Until* **Shiloh** *(Jesus) comes; and to Him shall be the obedience of the people.*
**Gen. 49:10** *(NKJV)* Emphasis added.

*Immediately I was in the Spirit; and behold, a throne set in heaven, and One sat on the throne.*
**Rev. 4:2** *(NKJV)*

Jesus looked to be about, 100,000 miles tall! The universe became frightened and bowed before Him, but the earth, rejoiced! In a blink of an eye, I was violently taken back to my living room. Christian, let me tell you. The fear of Jesus coming off His Throne was immensely omnipotent; way beyond you can ever imagine, or life can ever take you! His presence is fearful and very terrible! I am glad that I am on His side. I've experienced demonic fear like I have never known (I talk about that experience in chapter ten) but this surpasses anything conceivable. On a greater note, this kind of fear emitting from God's wrath and His verdict is tremendously intense, great, and dreadful when a child of disobedience is under it. Believe me saints; you do not want to stand around on the left side with the 'Goats' when His final ruling for a death sentence is to be passed on you. His Eyes Ablaze will fearfully pierce through your soul passing the depths of your spirit in raw judgment of His refiners fire. I fell on my face and started to cry while worshipping The Great God Yahweh, King of Unlimited Power! Saints, Jesus is real! Everything waits, asks permission, submits, and bows to Him. He doesn't have power He **is** Power! Power asks Jesus when to move! Unexplainable mysteries were given to me along with secrets unspeakable. It has been difficult to comprehend and yet I understand and at the same time to complex to write them down into the chapters of this book. Here are few small and very simple examples of what I mean:

He said, that He **is** *"The Forever."*

He communicated these words to me,

*"Son, I AM still expanding the universe so I could fit inside of it, since its creation, the universe is still a speck of air dust, trying to accommodate Me!"* (1 Kings 8:27).

*"Luis, I AM forever!"*

He continued,

*"I AM three forever's but one God."*

*"All things created work for me and serve Me, even Satan, I AM in control He does what I say."*

*"I never had a father or mother, I AM!"*

*"I AM never beneath, it doesn't exist."*

*"I speak water, and waves come to all shores of the land in fear and submission."*

*"I AM in the past, the present, and the future, all in the same Day, because tomorrow never comes it always is one Day."*

*"I move East, West, North, South in every direction at the same time, you can never fathom, and yet I move toward my children into one direction spiritually and physically hear their cry for my Son to save them!"*

*"I AM speaking to you now, also in your mothers womb, in the present as you live your life, and also the "you" in the future."*

*"My Name transforms the broken, the hurting, and the guilty. I restore and break down, I never "Rise," "Rise" waits for me to give it permission to do so."*

*"Deja'vu's are given, to show you predestination, you lived this life once before and then I seal the secret in the vastness of time you were created to borrow."*

*"I, The Resurrection, take the ashes of my children from all the scattered oceans and seas, will put them back together again on My Day in a blink of an eye."*

I don't know about you, but God is awesome and cannot be explained in human language. To me that is profound and ineffable.

He has fired flamed eyeballs, in His eye sockets! An actual sword for a tongue! The Book of Revelation expounds on some of these things, He revealed and spoke to me about. These were written just so it would encourage you.

For all those who forgot, we serve a GIGANTIC, SIZELESS, and ALL-Powerful GOD! It's so hard to find the words to explain it. When the Holy Spirit allowed me to see what was permissible, it amazed my entire being. The Scripture *is* true; the earth literally *is* His footstool! Praise God!

## DRAWN BY HIS SPIRIT

The Lord I know promised me new life and new life in full abundance. One thing that many in the Body of Christ don't seem to understand, is when you live "in this abundant life," more issues come your way. Jesus did promise us trials of fire, and tribulations until our end comes, whether it is in death or the rapture. In my own familiarity, I didn't hear the gospel message in my younger years, until I turned fifteen years old. As a small child ever since I could remember, I would hear about a man named Jesus doing all these great and powerful works and saying the most wonderful lexis a human being can ever hear. WOW!!! It knocked me off my feet because at fifteen years of age, God allowed me to hear it for the first time.

Occasionally, my spirit heard the Gospel message since I was kid in church with my grandmother, but my soul didn't hear it. Now I am aware of those impressions in my inner being on how God deals with us, by His Spirit and influence. The verse, which declares no one can come to Jesus unless God draws him, makes total and perfect sense when you think about it. In other words, you will not want Jesus at all until God tugs on your heart by the Holy Spirit—No tug, no Jesus. Like an explosion of fine comprehension entered my heart like never before, putting together what I have never clutched when others spoke about it. Even so in our human nature, we were given the will to choose Christ once He begins to draw us by tugging at our hearts with His Spirit. On the other side of the fence, we have the option to stay away from the Call of the Lord, which a lot of people have chosen to do. Rather, they walk down a lane, ignoring His voice, never promising absolution for their erroneous choices. Moreover, they can simply say 'Yes' to God and move forward for the King's Kingdom making a harmful impact on Satan's domain, but they chose to give into a reprobate mind instead. All those who denied Christ get a second chance in the Great Tribulation period, but it is certainly not guaranteed. Blessed are those in the first resurrection to prevent the second death to have power over you.

*No man can come to me, except the Father, which hath sent me draw, him.*
**John 6:44** *(KJV)*

*Blessed and holy is he who has part in the first resurrection. Over such the second death has no power…*
**Rev. 20:6** *(NKJV)*

Our hope is for the Lord to draw our loved ones, to say *yes* to the call of God on their lives, just like we did, so they could be saved and be with us in heaven for eternity. Not only does the enemy attack us in all unusual aspects in the seen and the unseen, but also because of the call on our lives for ministry. He also hates the fact that we look just like God.

*And God said; Let us make man in our image, after our likeness.*
**Gen. 1:26** *(KJV)*

In the original Hebrew text, "…*a little lower than* **Elohim**," is "…*a little lower than* **God**," which is the proper translation, not *"angels"* as we see in other versions. We are not created a little lower than the angels; besides, angels don't look like God—we do. You will never find that in the Holy Writ. Additionally, you will find that angels are described as flames of fire and ministering spirits. In fact, according to the Book of Enoch, "Uriel" is one of the Archangel's alongside Michael. Uriel's name means: "Flame of fire." I thought that was interesting to know. Nevertheless, he is not found in the Holy Manuscript of God. Angels were mystified when the Lord decided to create "Man," they couldn't comprehend and were baffled what a "Man" was until we came into existence.

*What is man, that thou art mindful of him? And the son of man, that thou visitest him? For thou hast made him but* **little lower than God***, and crownest him with glory and honor.*
**Psalms 8:4-5** *(ASV)* Emphasis added.

*Who makes His angels spirits, His ministers a flame of fire.*
**Psalms 104:4** *(NKJV)*

## HOLY SPIRIT, ARE YOU A PERSON?

In the world today, you will hear a lot of different opinions and beliefs about the Holy Spirit. Alongside Jesus, the Holy Spirit is next in line that gets attacked constantly. Millions believe He is an "It," a force, others believe He is a being of some sort and not personal. What they fail to understand, He is God of the third part of the trinity according to God the father, you can find that throughout the Old Testament expressively also in the first chapter of Genesis 1:26 since angels do not have the power to create anything. The Word of the Lord is ever present with specifics and details telling you exactly who is the Holy Spirit. If you thirst, He converts Himself into 'Water.'

If you hunger, He transforms into 'Bread.' If you are lonely and afraid, He converts into 'The Comforter.'

Like a gentle surgeon He opens up your heart and presents it to you exactly where it is. At first, it is uncomfortable and painful to see something you don't like about yourself. However, how would you grow and mature if the Lord does not represent and introduces you, to you. Looking into your own reflection will reveal what needs to be worked on in the deepest part of yourself, to bring out the *greatness* lying dormant within you.

## THE GENTLE SURGEON

When a man goes to a medical clinic for his yearly check up, and his personal doctor suggests that the patient must have open-heart surgery to receive an artificial one. Presumably when surgery is implemented, they get rid of the old heart and replace it with a new one. In contrast, when a sinner gives his or her life to the Lord, their old heart is taken away and then given a new one. Not only is their spirit born again, they also receive a heart that comes from the *"Living Water"* of God, which is the Holy Ghost. Ultimately, the new believer is susceptible and open to all miscellaneous attacks if not astute and perceptive. Like the medical patient who received his new heart, if he were to come back ten years later for his old heart, his doctor would think his patient is crazy after a decade has gone by. Jesus made this very clear, when the Bible tells us; we all have an evil spirit living inside of us. And when the evil spirit leaves because Jesus' Spirit enters in, he will leave for a season and then returns to see if the person is still saved. If the Image Bearer backslides into a fallen state—meaning no longer serving the Lord in obedience to His will—The evil spirit he had prior, will go get seven others more wicked than itself and re-enters into him.

*When an unclean spirit goes out of a man, he goes through dry places, seeking rest, and finds none. Then he says, 'I will return to my house from which I came.' And when he comes, he finds it empty, swept, and put in order. Then he goes and takes with him seven other spirits more-wicked than himself, and they enter and dwell there; and the last state of that man is worse than the first. So shall it also be with this wicked generation.*
**Matt. 12:43-45** *(NKJV)*


## THE BIGGEST LOSER


Eventually, as the days go by we tend to resist the Spirit of God on a lot of different levels, which happens to all of us on an each day basis. The *Living Water* I write about is the proof on the earth for all men to realize there is a real spiritual battle going on in the supernatural. Most men of God had tried to grab hold in what was already foretold and ran with it, while others grab hold to the world and live in it to the best of their ability. Hence, as Christians we see very clearly and no longer blind to the mayhem of the devil's onslaught, we have to walk in conformity with the Holy Ghost. Fighting a defeated foe has to be done with wisdom, you cannot war with someone who is already defeated. As a nation of sanctified people, we battle flies with bazookas, and crickets with rocket launchers. In my mind, I believe that is too much artillery for something so small and probably insignificant to encounter with such weapons. Prioritize yourself to put your situations in perspective and balance. Bring it to the throne room of God and fight yourself to keep it at His doorsteps, especially if the situation or burden is too heavy to carry. Walking away from certain proclivities the enemy might throw at you, knowing it could bring some type of relief is wise. All things considered, even though Satan is the god of this world, he is the loser in all areas of your life, they only way he isn't the biggest loser is if you give him the upper hand. I challenge you today to take into consideration not to leave your spirit unguarded. Don't give Satan so much credit. Remember its not always the devil doing it, sometimes its just you, he just intensifies what you already was thinking from the start.

*The **god of this world** has blinded the minds of those who don't believe. As a result, they don't see the light of the Good News about Christ's glory. It is Christ who is God's image.*
**2 Cor. 4:4** *(Gods Word)* Emphasis added.

*Come to Me, all you who labor and are heavy laden, and I will give you rest. Take My yoke upon you and learn from Me, for I am gentle and lowly in heart, and you will find rest for your souls. For My yoke is easy and My burden is light."*
**Matt. 11:28-30** *(NKJV)*


## CHRISTIANS CANNOT BE DEMON POSSESSED

Jesus in His Word, made it evident about addressing this contentious issue of, "Christians can be demon possessed." The Lord wants the record straight, since He did not give us His Spirit whom is weak and feeble, NEVER! The Holy Word doesn't validate a person born from above, with the Holy Spirit living on the inside of their spirit, to become demon possessed. Christ desires everyone to know that the Living Water is not susceptible to Satan at any given time. When a born again Christian has the Spirit of the Lord dwelling on the inside of his human spirit, the devil or any of his legions, princes, or generals do not have the power, to come into him and take the Holy Spirit out of his body when Satan feels like it. It then defeats and contradicts many passages of Scripture stating that the Holy Spirit in you is Greater than the one who is in the world—Satan, who is the god of this world. God's Word cannot come to fullness in your reality, if, Christ in you is **not** the hope of glory, or have less power then our enemy. I believe a Christian can be repressed, suppressed, depressed, oppressed, but **not** possessed. Nevertheless, many will believe that Christians can be possessed by devils regardless what anyone says, on the other side of that mental reasoning, if a believer were to be possessed, at some degree, it was because their disobedience and willingness to fall away (See Jude vs 24). Again, as you also read in the 'Gentle Surgeon', I re-iterate:

*But if I, by the finger of God, send out evil spirits, then the kingdom of God has overtaken you. When the strong man armed keeps watch over his house, then his goods are safe: But when one who is stronger makes an attack on him and overcomes him, he takes away his instruments of war, in which he had put his faith, and makes division of his goods. He who is not with me is against me, and he who will not give me help in getting people together is driving them away. The unclean spirit, when he has gone out of a man, goes through dry places, looking for rest; and when he does not get it, he says, I will go back to my house from which I came. And when he comes, he sees that it has been made fair and clean. Then he goes and gets seven other spirits more evil than himself, and they go in, and take their places there: and the last condition of that man is worse than the first.*
**Luke 11:20-26** *(Bible in Basic English)*

Factually, this process will not occur simply because they were doing right in the sight of God, but for the reason the believer was dabbing with continual and non-repented sin. Thus, opening the door for the Spirit of God to leave, therefore, the unclean spirit can return back to its original host—You. Fortunately, "Greater is He who is in you, then he who is in the world," live by the Word, stand by the Word, at all times, do not let your guard down!

*And* **the Spirit of the Lord came mightily upon him**, *and he tore the lion apart*
**Judges 14:6** *(NKJV)* Emphasis added.

*Behold, I send the Promise of My Father upon you; but tarry in the city of Jerusalem until you are **endued with power from on high**."*
**Luke 24:49** *(NKJV)* Emphasis added.

*That he would grant you, according to the riches of his glory, **to be strengthened with might by his Spirit in the inner man**...*
**Eph. 3:16** *(KJV)* Emphasis added.

*...**Christ in you**, the hope of glory.*
**Col. 1:27** *(NKJV)* Emphasis added.

*For our gospel did not come to you in word only, **but also in power, and in the Holy Spirit** and in much assurance, as you know what kind of men we were among you for your sake.*
**1 Thess. 1:5** *(NKJV)* Emphasis added.

*For God has not given us a spirit of fear, **but of power** and of love and of a sound mind.*
**2 Tim. 1:7** *(NKJV)* Emphasis added.

*...**Greater is He that is in you**, than he that is in the world.*
**1 John 4:4 (KJV)** Emphasis added.


Stand strong in Christ by the supreme power of the Holy Ghost, He will never allow you to stay comfortless. In your times of need is when He shows Himself strong. Always retain a thirst for the Living Water.

# CAN THE REAL CHRISTIAN PLEASE STAND UP?

# Chapter Ten

## CAN THE REAL CHRISTIAN PLEASE STAND UP?

*Hypocrite! First remove the plank from your
own eye, and then you will see clearly to
remove the speck from your brother's eye.*

**—Matthew 7:5**

NOVEMBER 2002, ON A COLD SATURDAY night. I was sitting
in my living room reading my Bible. It was already late and
the kids were sleeping in their bedroom. My wife kissed
me goodnight and decided to go to bed early in order to
have enough time for church service the next morning. I
paused for a moment from reading, and went ahead to go
check the backdoor of the house to make sure it was locked.
When coming back from making sure the backdoor was
locked, my wife already had entered into the bedroom and
closed the door behind her. While returning to the living
room I continued reading where I left off. While reading, an
overwhelming feeling came over me making me feel drained,
tired, and sleepy. It felt like a spirit of slumber was hovering
over me causing me to hit the pillow earlier, plus it was getting
late, so I desist from thinking that it was a spirit of slumber
and decided to go to sleep on the couch, thinking nothing
of it. For some reason the Spirit of God kept pushing me to

continue reading and I noticed that it was 1:50am. Exhausted as I was, I knew to pray before I became too sleepy and not able to pray to the Lord.

Not able to specifically recall every detail, but I remember turning the light off and laying back on the sofa with my right arm over my eyes and began praying, then, I think a few seconds went by when suddenly, I sat back up again. The odd thing was, I didn't feel tired, sleepy, or exhausted, before I fell asleep. As I stood up from the sofa, I saw my body stiff as a mannequin, just lying in the same position with my right arm over my eyes as when I fell asleep, but with no breath (being separated, from my body felt more real then this life). It felt so unusual; my senses were heightening by the minute, to the extent I was able to hear a whisper of someone speaking in the country of Australia, from my home in New York. I could feel the atmosphere and the air moving in me and through me. My soul was able to touch the walls and the air itself without me literally touching it. About this time I am in awe, captivated that my five senses became seven and magnified fifty thousand times over! If I wanted to go through the ceiling or through the floor I knew I had that power, traveling at the speed of thought was pure normalcy. Great distance is not an issue in the spirit realm, and eternity is understood in its fullness. I had to paint a mental picture for you in words to give you an idea how long eternity is in our finite minds, knowing this will never be enough to comprehend the endless.

## HOW LONG IS ETERNITY?

While this was going on I comprehended what eternity feels like. Oh my goodness! We have not a centimeter of a clue how long is infinity. You don't understand eternity in these mortal bodies, but you come to FULL understanding what it feels like when you are out of your earthen vessel, it is a very, very long endless perpetuity, time is no more. Pictorially, I will illustrate a mental image to help broaden the perspective of endless duration the best I can. Lets say the whole earth is a planet of just ocean, just a large humongous mass of pure ocean many miles deep. And you have a small finch fly every one trillion years across our known universe, flying through countless galaxies to earth and when the small finch gets to earth there is a small piece of land he stands on to have a little drop of water, and then fly back to its original destination. Now this little bird will continuously do this until he drinks the very last drop of the entire planets water supply until dry, and that is when eternity begins. I don't know about you, but this is the best mental picture I could describe to explain the enormity of eternity. That is a long time to fathom.

## UNINVITED VISITOR

Realizing that my wife was in the room sleeping and so were the kids, I was not afraid, and knew they were safe. As I was turning around, about one hundred and eighty degrees to my left, I see a huge, tall, dark, black figure, about twelve feet from me just standing there in half. What I mean by half was that half of his body was visible and the other half was inside the wall. I mean the blackest of the blackest you can ever imagine! You can be in the darkest room with a blindfold and your hands over your eyes; it will not be dark or black enough. You could feel his darkness! I was petrified, the fear was indescribable, and it was horrific. It reminded me of Moses when God used him to manifest His wonders in Egypt, when he mentions a darkness that can be felt, I believe this was similar. *Then the LORD said to Moses, "Stretch out your hand toward heaven, that there may be darkness over the land of Egypt, darkness which may even be felt." So Moses stretched out his hand toward heaven, and there was thick darkness in all the land of Egypt three days."* Exodus 10:21-22 (NKJV). Saints, the fear that emanated from this dark figure was unexplainable. Imagine taking all your fears you have ever experienced, combining it with all the fears of the world. Magnifying it, about one thousand times, it will not match the fear that came from this thing. I was forced to keep my eyes on him. He was hurting my vision because I could touch his fear with my eyes! I was so afraid! But the fear did not enter into me, yet I felt my senses tremble. The fear of the Lord was more powerful inside me in comparison with the fear of the enemy, its insignificant. Instantaneously, before I had a chance to think, a voice inside of me whispered, which I knew was the Holy Spirit saying, "That's him, that's Satan." (Sarcastically) I thought, "Oh…great!" Immediately, Satan then began to speak in a language I never heard before. Those words he spoke were not of this earth. I heard him speak into my left ear, only. I just wanted this to stop! It sounded like gibberish, like he was blaming me for something. He was pointing his fingers toward me but yet not moving. Notably, he didn't have human fingers, but a black and dark human figured body. I couldn't understand it. I was prevented from understanding "The Language of evil spirits," in order to keep me safe and protected.

# THE UNEXPLAINABLE

A strong feeling of hatred came from him, and I realized that he really hated me. I am speaking from a perspective of a profound hatred not known to man, **demon**strating to me like I was in his way. If I were to translate it into words, its like saying, "I hate you get out of my line of attacks you are hindering me." At that moment, he begins to get closer, and the closer he got the weaker I became, and the more evil in the room intensified! His voice, hatred, anger, and accusations became stronger and louder. As he kept moving, floating closer to me, like electricity from every area of my body started to shoot out from within me to the outside of my spirit. (I apologize but it's really difficult to explain the supernatural into earth language, to express the ineffable). Even as the electricity started pulsating from the inside of me, Satan moved back quickly, like he was losing power and strength. Next, quickly he raises his right arm and I was violently sent back into my body. When it happened I saw my "breath of lives" (Literal Greek translation) return to me. My soul and spirit sat up first and my body followed after, and then *we* (body, soul, spirit) were one again (1 Thess. 5:23).

I began to yell at the top of my voice. "Help Me! Help Me! As soon as I came to myself, praying was the first thing that popped into my mind. Rebuking Satan by telling him he had no right to show himself to me. My wife was startled out of her sleep with all the commotion going on. She pushed the bedroom door open really fast and it hit against the wall, BAAAM! And she began to shout, "Honey, honey what's wrong!" "Talk to me you're scaring me." "What happened?" Although she was speaking, I was speechless. I couldn't talk, but prayed while rocking back and forth on the couch in the living room. Whispering to myself prayers to fight against the fear I have felt and the evil that was with me. It was 2:50am. So this tells me, this occurrence kept its peak for about twenty-five minutes. Not being able to really hear anyone but myself praying, my wife just sat next to me holding me and comforting me until peace ruled me. Frantically, I tried calling my friends for counsel, but I just couldn't grab hold of the phone, it kept falling out of my hands from all the shaking. Everything around me was faded away. Eventually, the Lord touched my spirit and told me to be peaceful; and I was able to explain the event of what just happened, to my wife.

## REVELATION KNOWLEDGE OF EVIL DOMINION COUNTERPOWERS

The Holy Spirit revealed to me a diminutive revelation. As we all know, the understanding of the supernatural when pertaining to demons and evil spirits, they have names, ranks, sizes, and function in chaotic order, under the influence of Satan who has the spirit of devil. Satan has generals and powers of the air at work for him, here are their names; you might be familiar with some of these: Belial, Onokian (a general, he hovers over Iran), Azazel goat (goat like demon, Leviticus 16:8-10), Spawn, Python (divination, Acts 16), Oni, Beelzebub, Octopus, general demons, Cormorant, Uzza, Azzael, Marine-water spirits, animalistic spirits, the Screeching Owl, spirit of Pan (causes humans to have panic attacks) foul spirits, unclean spirits, infirmity spirits and countless others I can't write, they are in the millions! Believe me saints; you do not want to see them or be confronted by any! These are principalities, powers, rulers in high places, and of the earth.

Whether unsaved or saved they will manifest and harass you. If the devil were not bothering you at all whatsoever, then I would consider my walk with Christ, and make sure that it is a genuine legitimate walk. If you are not doing anything to put a spiritual dent and void into the kingdom of darkness, then something has to be wrong if there is no threat on your behalf against Satan to cause him to go into an uproar.

Anyone who experienced a foul stench in their home, maybe in the bedroom or the living room, the first thought is someone must have eaten something that might not had fallen right in their stomach. Probably, one of the kids or someone else used the bathroom, or the garbage wasn't thrown out, or maybe something is cooking that doesn't have a pleasant scent. And these are all legitimate reasons for such odors. But one in particular has been manifested when we know the plumbing pipes of the toilet are not busted, and that is rulers of this dark world: This is when you need to be courageous and walking in the Spirit's power to be able to stand up to these supernatural spirits, because you are being visited. The stench is so foul its like rotting flesh and feces burning at the same time, but this a foul smelling spirit that comes out of hell from the center of the earth.

*Principalities and Powers in high places;* these wicked beings come from the second heaven. Many years ago, I had a roommate who was a born again Christian, him and I would always make it a priority after work to get into the Word and have a Bible study or go to mid-week service together. One day when coming home late from work, as I was entering the front door, he told me frantically, we needed to pray that very moment. When he said this, he sounded a little freaked out as well.

*Reminder:* the experience below was years before I had my encounter with Satan, I only understood a little of the supernatural.

I asked him, "What's going on are you okay?"

He said, "No, I am not okay, I never witnessed something like this before."

I replied, "Witness what, what happened to you?

(*Stammering*)
He answered,

"When, I entered my bedroom to place my books on the table and walk toward the bed, the room temperature went completely cold like it was the middle of winter."

(*Slowly*)
I responded,

"Reeeaaally?" I knew he was a new believer and thought maybe he was joking with me, but as he went on I could tell from his body language that he was telling me the truth, seeing he was really frightened and confused about the whole matter.

He continued,

"Luis, I know you taught me about what the Bible says about demonic realms and evil spirits and all of those crazy things, but I didn't think any of it was real. Man, I was able to see my breath it was so cold Lou, like it was 5 degrees in here, what really freaked me out, was the fact only my room was that cold, and just three feet from my bedroom door, I could step into the living room and it was hot, and so was your room!"

I replied, "Alexci, what did you do?"

Alexci responds authoritatively,

"Well, I felt a heaviness in the room and knew that these cold spirits were lingering with me. I had an overwhelming presence of fear and evil surrounding me, so I stomped my right foot on the floor as hard as I could and said in a loud voice, "In the name of Jesus! I rebuke you demons of hell, go back to where you came from, you don't belong in my house, my home is the house of my God!"

The end result of this episode is when he stomped on the floor and rebuked the spirits that were in his room, he believed they went back from whence they came, and the temperature gradually returned to normal.

If it were the middle of winter, I would have thought nothing of it, guessing he might have left his window open, but this occurred in the middle of July. It was 84 degrees, hot and humid. I didn't understand what was the difference from the foul spirits and when rooms get cold as demons would visit people, until later on in my walk. Reader, if you have experienced something similar in your personal life or had a shared experience with someone else at this level or greater, then you were just visited by a principality in *high places*, and that *high place* is the second heaven which we call "Space." To give you a small synopsis of how cold space is, its negative -463 degrees below zero. (Selah) Now that is beyond what we know about how cold freezing is, incomprehensible. Car gas you put in your vehicle freezes at negative -150 degrees, imagine that for a moment compared to outerspace.

So when these evil principality spirits come down to earth since they roam up and down from earth to the heavens, as they travel, asking permission to accuse and harass us, they adapt to our environment. When they visit humans they can also affect the environment around them, causing it to become what they need it to be to accommodate them to be comfortable leaving a residue where they've been and dwell.

## CAREFUL WITH ASSUMPTIONS

After a few minutes went by, I explained the whole thing to my wife. The kids did not wake up at all during this whole time I am explaining the situation, prior to the yelling. This whole ordeal was indescribable. I tell you the truth, anyone who would have gone through what happened to me, there would not be one atheist, agnostic, unbeliever or backslider in the world that will doubt that God or the Devil exists. Not one doubt at ALL! Explaining this account to the populace, they would say it was only a figment of my imagination and that none of it was real, it was all in my head, and just a nightmare. Certainly, there will be those who believe and would not wish this experience or anything similar to happen to them. Regrettably, I shared this with a few people. And they presupposed something was wrong with me. Inopportunely, not everyone understands the supernatural and why things happen to them or someone they know. As humans we tend to label everything, and stay away from the unknown. If I wasn't a real Holy Ghost filled Christian, I believe Satan would have done a lot more damage than I could ever imagine.

I acknowledged earlier, Jesus was asking His disciples, "Who do you say, that I am?" Jesus discerned, that His character was being questioned. The religious people of that day did not understand the call on His life, and who He really was. They condemned the Lord because of the unfamiliar and for being a son of a known carpenter, instead of the Son of God. If they took the time to understand Jesus, they would have known that Jesus was the "child that's born" who is the Son of man, and Christ is the "son given" who is the Son of God. Alas, it never turned out that way for them, having the focus on humanity, in turn it worked out for our good so we can have the opportunity to enter heaven. We must be cautious in all instances knowing the devil is always at work and never sleeps since he's a spirit so is the Spirit of Christ, but one will always be in our favor. Not all will accept who you are and you know this, are you able to stand when your reputation is judged? Will you stand for Christ and not be ashamed as they did in times past?

Believe me, just like it proceeded with Jesus, you and I will be judged and talked about for numerous amounts of unusual things. Its up to you to hold on to what God put in front of you with a fire that can never be rancid, whether you had a vision, a dream, or an experience. Keep walking into the destiny, which was hand painted and sculpted for your life. We will be misunderstood at times and condemned for things that are not in our control, but my counsel to you, would be, hold on with hope, faith, and trust in the Lord with much prayer! All of this happened just a little while later, after I accepted the Call of God into my life. Saints, *easy* will not be the words to describe the entire walk of an Image Bearer, but its possible to walk with the power of the Spirit, as we listen to His voice as a continual normalcy. Satan will try to prevent and slow you down, but know this, he could prevent us only if we listen to his voice and reject the voice of the Spirit of God. Satan knows damage will come to his kingdom if you are aware of who you are in Jesus.

## THE WORLD'S COUNTING ON US

Hopefully, God's Word helps you or someone you know to stay in obedience. My heart aches when I think about the billions of people that will not make it into heaven. Billions in false religions and secular humanism open minded for all different kinds of methods and ideologies to get to God. 1.4 Billion Muslims, 1.5 Billion Catholics, 18 million Jehovah Witnesses, 11 million Mormons. That is an enormous community who are deceived in believing a lie; this is only mentioning a few.

There are 2.2 billion professing Christians today, but out of this vast number only 684 million are professing to be born again, according to statistics.

Here's a basic background on these false religions that I've mentioned:

▶ **Islam** – believes that Jesus is only a prophet, a good man, not God incarnate or the Son of God. Allah does not have a Son, according to the Qu'ran. [2 John 7-11; 1 John. 4:1-6; & Proverbs 30:4] There is a major difference between the Elijah Muhammad that the Nation of Islam teaches as being the last prophet in the sixties as opposed to the Mohammad from 7th century Arabia. In my short period of being Muslim per se, I realized the two did not agree with each other about a lot of things.

▶ **Catholicism** – believes works gets you to heaven, and that you can pray to Mary to get to Jesus. In recent years the Vatican received 4.1 million petitions to make Mary part of the trinity [1 Tim. 2:5]. "Wouldn't that be a quadrilogy?" In Latin, "Vatis" means *Divine* or *Prophetic* and "Can," means *Serpent* or *Snake*. (*Vatiscan = Divine prophetic serpent and snake*). Idol worshippers are an abomination to the Lord, and we must be very meticulous in how we handle ourselves accordingly.

▶ **Jehovah Witness** – don't believe in Heaven or Hell. There is no Holy Spirit living inside believers. The Holy Spirit is just a force. Michael and Jesus are created beings. Jesus is not God, but **A** Son of God. He is "**A** Word," not "**The** Word." [Jn. 1:1, Rev. 3:20 & Jn. 3:3-8]

▶ **Mormons** – baptize their members in the name of the dead. They believe that their church has a group of men and women in the "spirit world" who are spreading the Mormon gospel to the dead who have not received an opportunity to convert to Mormonism. And when they do say 'Yes' to this conversion, they also get baptized in the name of the dead. [Matt. 28:19 & Acts 2:38]

Fallen souls, with a fallen ministry, living in a fallen world, with a fallen mentality, will cause you to fall many times.

*I marvel that you are turning away so soon from Him who called you in the grace of Christ, to a different gospel, which is not another; but there are some who trouble you and want to pervert the gospel of Christ. But even if we, or an angel from heaven, preach any other gospel to you than what we have preached to you, let him be accursed. As we have said before, so now I say again, if anyone preaches any other gospel to you than what you have received, let him be accursed. For do I now persuade men, or God? Or do I seek to please men? For if I still pleased men, I would not be a bondservant of Christ. But I make known to you, brethren that the gospel, which was preached by me, is not according to man. For I neither received it from man, nor was I taught it, but it came through the revelation of Jesus Christ.*
**Gal. 1:6-12** *(NKJV)*

## STAND FOR HOLINESS

If you claim to be a real Christian who loves God with all of your heart, then I would tell you to stand up and proclaim the Good News from the housetops and let everyone know that Jesus is Lord! Helping and assisting others prepare themselves for the coming King is our primary objective to the highest degree. Only one way can get you ready for the presence of Almighty God, and that is having an attitude of repentance, repentance is the key to eternal life. My prayer for you is that you will always allow the ardor of God and the certainty of His Word to resonate Love, true worship, and forgiveness alongside obedience and repentance to reign in your mortal bodies. And let it also reign in your soul, thus, the Spirit can truly live and give God the worship through you, which He definitely and rightly deserves. We just have to get back up and not stay in the situation. Keep on keeping on, never giving up knowing that God will never give up on you! Take a stand!

*Draw near to God and He will draw near to you.*
**James 4:8** *(NKJV)*

**Stand fast** *therefore in the liberty by which Christ has made us free, and do not be entangled again with a yoke of bondage.*
**Gal. 5:1** *(NKJV)* Emphasis added

*Put on the whole armor of God, that you may be able to* **stand** *against the wiles of the devil.*
**Eph. 6:11** *(NKJV)* Emphasis added.

*Therefore take up the whole armor of God, that you may be able to* **withstand** *in the evil day, and having done all, to stand.* **Stand therefore**, *having girded your waist with truth, having put on the breastplate of righteousness…*
**Eph. 6:13-14** *(NKJV)* Emphasis added.

*…So* **stand fast** *in the Lord, beloved.*
**Phil. 4:1** *(NKJV)* Emphasis added.

*Therefore, brethren,* **stand fast** *and hold the traditions, which you were taught, whether by word or our epistle. Now may our Lord Jesus Christ Himself, and our God and Father, who has loved us and given us everlasting consolation and good hope by grace…*
**2 Thess. 2:15-16** *(NKJV)* Emphasis added.

## MAKE A STAND AND GET INVOLVED

To live under the shadow of "The Almighty," is an exciting journey (Psalms 91:1, 2). However, this journey will be short if you don't have the necessary tools to consistently be itinerant with the Lord to help you build that one on one relationship, in order to have the blessings and promises come to manifestation. Saints that don't pray and seek after God, as they should, are carnal Christians. Never walking in the spirit wondering what is going on, complaining to their spouses and friends: "Why the blessings of God are trickling in, instead of raining in, like everybody says?" I tell you the truth, if you have trouble walking, 'the walk of Life with Christ,' then you need to be more involved and learn to give yourself away. Pay your tithes and offerings, give, sow seed, and watch God move mightily in your life and your finances, in this life now! One of many reasons we have to pay our tithes, is to primarily break the back of this satanic stingy spirit, which has a hold on many of us, preventing many from learning to become givers and not takers only. Multitudes of Christians do not have a problem paying out of pocket to attend worldly music concerts, for all sorts of personal desires, high priced restaurants, and various events. People of God, do not be this way, if you happen to be walking on this unruly path, get off quickly! In fact, the Lord God told me in regards of giving to His work and the church, "Luis, my people could give their tithes and offerings to Me forever, and it will never amount to My giving of My only Son who died on the cross for you and for them!" You must learn to give not only money, but also your time away to others as well as spending time with God, and watch God spend time with you. Give and it shall be given to you; keep, and it shall be kept from you. This law is for the singles and the married. In fact, singles and married couples should get connected and engage themselves into a cell group or maybe a ministry with their local church, and find out if there is anything you can do to serve the Lord and His people. Serve your pastor, and ask if you can be placed in a position that can help him in the ministry or others in need, that pertains to the church or out-reach ministry, if available.

There are thousands out their waiting on you, waiting to be blessed by your spiritual gifts.

There are believers in the Body of Christ who can appreciate the anointing on your life to bless and encourage others. But if you happen to be the one having trouble in your marriage, I would encourage you and your spouse to investigate, if there is marital counseling available—do not do this alone, particularly if you are single. Assuredly, another couple in leadership, ordained by the pastor who is stronger in the Lord then you, can come in and help mend your marriage by executing holy and righteous order. Always be in a state of mind of being accountable to your leaders, and you will go far with your walk with Christ and your marriage will prosper, and so will the single people.

*Beloved, I pray that you may prosper in all things and be in health, just as your soul prospers.*
**3 John 1:2** *(NKJV)*


## SERVANTHOOD

There is nothing like a man or woman who knows how to serve and submit, under His shade. We do not have enough couples or single people going out there witnessing and helping the church and their leaders with ministry duties. This is our job, we are to work and occupy until Jesus' eminent return. Even though I am an apostle of the Lord Jesus Christ, I am a servant first, titles, we can do away with, their are times these titles are important but it cannot be the all around sum total of a man, if he doesn't know how to serve the Lord and those who inhabit the earth, then he has much to learn. Always striving to make sure I walk with a reputation in God's eyes as His friend. People in churches sing these songs to the Lord, clapping, shouting, singing I am a "friend of God," and

He doesn't even know them. They must repent and examine themselves so God can come in and heal them where they hurt, or where they lack in holiness, for without holiness no one will see the Lord.


## STAND FOR PERFECTION

When you start to get involved in ministry you will meet a lot of different and interesting people. As we stride for perfection in Christ and seek His face, the believer must be aware who is in their loop of interest. If you are single, by no means I would tell you, go out with a person you like, alone, that is just a snare and a trap. Be astute; keep from putting yourself in a position or a quandary that can cause you to fall in sin. Be wise as a serpent and gentle as a dove, again, staying away from the appearance of evil. If you do not follow the Word of God, as we all should, you will lose yourself in the process, and then finding excuses why you are in the position that you are in to justify your means. Ironically, you will find multitudes of men and women in the church you would minister to over and over again, and no matter how simple the message it never gets across. Many times the Lord says that He would give them over to a reprobate mind if they continue in this manner. That's Bible, **not** Luis Lopez 101.

*Let no one deceive you by any means;* ***for that Day will not come unless the falling away comes first,*** *and the man of sin is revealed, the son of perdition, who opposes and exalts himself above all that is called God or that is worshiped, so that he sits as God in the temple of God, showing himself that he is God. Do you not remember that when I was still with you I told you these things? And now you know what is restraining, that he may be revealed in his own time.* ***For the mystery of lawlessness is already at work*** *only He who now restrains will do so until He is taken out of the way. And then the lawless one will be revealed, whom the Lord*

*will consume with the breath of His mouth and destroy with the brightness of His coming.* **The coming of the lawless one is according to the working of Satan, with all power, signs, and lying wonders,** *and with all unrighteous deception among those who perish, because they did not receive the love of the truth, that they might be saved.* **And for this reason God will send them strong delusion, that they should believe the lie, that they all may be condemned who did not believe the truth but had pleasure in unrighteousness.**
*2 Thess. 2:3-12 (NKJV)* Emphasis added.

You can't constantly reject Jesus Christ and the finish work of the cross for years at a time and not go through much disorder and dissension, in view of the fact that the adversary will not let up, he doesn't want you to be saved or repent from your backslidden state. Real liberty only subsists in the arms of Christ; while Satan's wicked agenda is making sure you are unable to. Caution yourself to never give into a reprobate mentality, and in that way God will prevent you from giving into a strong delusion in these final days we live in, and fulfill this prophecy. Today is the day of salvation for them who are lost or have fallen away; I say come back before its too late!

Evidently, if you are having difficulty being in Christ, or maybe you knew the Lord and have fallen away, go to a confidant you trust to help you be strong in God, with the assurance an accountability partner will make certain you will not wane to the left or the right. No one is Jesus, Jr. The devil tries to deceive us in thinking we could do it all by ourselves, transporting thoughts into us to become isolated from everyone else. Remember that, "isolation brings separation, but integration brings combination." This is exactly what you need, to combine with other believers in agreement and put 10,000 to flight, more than that now, knowing we have Jesus under the New Covenant of love and grace with further authority. No matter who you are, single, married, or engaged, when you are broken and humble, you always know how to put your pride to the side and run after what is right in the sight of the Lord. The 'giving' of *yourself* is important in the Body of Christ. It may not always be easy, but possible.

Typically, its with your time, money, love–you name it–the list goes on and on, concerning the abidance in God's will and plan for your destiny. The point will be, we don't want to *inhabit a place* to always take and not give, to be a reservoir and not a channel for blessings. There is a difference between, receiving and taking in all relationships, especially in marriage. Think about that for a moment. When we are in need we must sow. You reap what you give away. Stand strong in the Lord and follow after His Word. Believe me, serving others brings humility and a joy beyond what your heart can bear. A servant leader is a good leader. A lot of people want to lead; then again no one wants to ever serve. (That is a head scratcher). Lets keep together; walk in agreement with affection, especially with those of the house of the Lord. Why? Wolves hunt in packs and they wait for the sheep to stray away alone and then attack and kill them, sometimes very slowly. Basically, when we push those who are on the fence eventually they will fall on the wrong side, what they really need is that extra pull to the right side, if not, the evil one will come and take them away from the flock.

*Not forsaking the assembling of ourselves together, as is the manner of some, but exhorting one another, and so much the more as you see the Day approaching.*
**Heb. 10:25** *(NKJV)*

*Can two walk together, except they be agreed?*
**Amos 3:3** *(KJV)*

*For he who sows to his flesh will of the flesh reap corruption, but he who sows to the Spirit will of the Spirit reap everlasting life. And let us not grow weary while doing good, for in due season we shall reap if we do not lose heart. Therefore, as*

*we have opportunity,* **let us do good to all**, *especially to those who are of the household of faith.*
**Gal. 6:8-10** *(NKJV)* Emphasis added.

## STAND ON THE SURE WORD OF GOD

There are over 5,750 manuscripts written in relation to our history. The Sacred Word, is the most quoted of all, to the extreme point if you were to take all the quotes from every book ever written and combine them, you would have the entire Old and New Testament, accept for eleven verses. There's no faking that this Holy Book we follow is fake or altered in favor of those who say it is counterfeit. Such people walk in a spirit of error. We are standing on a sure word of prophecy and a very solid foundation. Peter said it best:

*And so we have the prophetic word confirmed, which you do well to heed as a light that shines in a dark place, until the day dawns and the morning star rises in your hearts; knowing this first, that no prophecy of Scripture is of any private interpretation, for prophecy never came by the will of man, but holy men of God spoke as they were moved by the Holy Spirit.*
**2 Peter 1:19-21** *(NKJV)*

### STAND FOR HOPE

The reason I named this chapter "Let the real Christian please stand up?" because a host of believers who do not take God seriously, are not standing up for the Lord as they should and are afraid. Jesus has done so much for humanity; we will never be able to pay him back for what He has done but only by the giving of our lives to Him, completely, sacrificially, and obediently. We must stand through adversity, weathering storms with vigor in the direction of holiness. Yet again, without holiness we will *not* see the Lord. We must stand fast when false religions begin to rise and try to contradict and shred down the Word for the truth it contains, while they are promoting a lie. Not all roads lead to heaven, even though one out of three Christians thinks so. Four hundred times the Bible says, Jesus is the **only** living truth, way, and resurrection, giving life to all who believe in Him, and we recognize the words He spoke as pure unadulterated truth. Jesus said, *"I am the way, the truth, and the life. No one comes to the Father except through Me."* John 14:6 (NKJV).

## DATES DID NOT CHANGE FOR OTHERS

Take note: All religions work hard to make their way to God, when Jesus has already done the work for us and established it, to redeem us back to our Father. If other religions are so true in their ways, why do they accept each other? Why all other religious books quote the Bible but the Bible never quotes other books? Many religious figures came and are now gone. Jesus Christ the Son of God and Man died, causing the acknowledged timeline to change. We concede to the acronym, B.C. and A.D., to be **A**nno **D**omini, Latin for: "In the year of our Lord" and B.C., **B**efore **C**hrist. When these religious people of the past passed away, the timeline never changed for them, or acknowledged them. The world caught on and decided to use B.C.E. and C.E., **B**efore **C**ommon **E**ra & **C**ommon **E**ra, trying to eradicate the truth of God's fingerprint on humanity. The minute you mention Jesus in a conversation the fight is on. The devil knew this truth, so he created many religions to make it difficult and confusing for anyone to desire the only True and living God. We must take the kingdom of God by force and stand for Jesus, even at the brink of a life and death situation. Jesus has been the most talked about, the most controversial; the most fought over individual of all, in the history of mankind, on top of the wars for Israel and Jerusalem the "City of the Great King." When Israel became a Nation on May 14th 1948–after 2,534 years when Israel didn't exist since Nebuchadnezzar– took control of Jerusalem in 1967, they have been attacked over 6,000 times. And these two events are prophetic in our history, these are the super signs Jesus talked about regarding the fig tree intertwined with His eminent return to earth in invisible form–The Rapture.

## EXAMINE YOURSELF

"Stop being so spiritual and religious," is the trademark and justification of the carnal and the counterfeit Christian, when in fact they need to examine themselves and also stop eating the Holy Communion every month at church in an unworthy manner, or judgment of death and/or sickness will fall on them. Especially when they are not walking in ignorance.

*Therefore whoever eats this bread or drinks this cup of the Lord in an*

*unworthy manner will be guilty of the body and blood of the Lord. But let a man examine himself, and so let him eat of the bread and drink of the cup. For he who eats and drinks in an unworthy manner eats and drinks judgment to himself, not discerning the Lord's body. For this reason many are weak and sick among you, and many sleep. For if we would judge ourselves, we would not be judged. But when we are judged, we are chastened by the Lord, that we may not be condemned with the world.*
**1 Cor. 11:27-32** *(NKJV)*

Jesus is watching every step you and I walk on earth, clueless to what will become of them in the future. We have to pray to make sure we get on the ball, prayer is very important if we want our loved ones to be led to salvation. But those who are playing church, walking with the knowledge of who Christ is must pray and in the same course, stay away from them, if not, Satan will use them for your ill will. The Christian must get it together so we could erect the kingdom of Christ for the glory of God the Father, and His Holy Spirit.

As a holy people we must stand against the devil and his legions, forbid yourself to let your guard down for a moment. No matter where we are or where we go, we have to stand and fight for what is right in the sight of the Lord at all times, the best we know how. Prayer is a very important weapon and will change all circumstances if you are consistent. As a righteous community of believers, we have to come against complacency and mediocrity. The Lord desires for us to prosper and be in health, to build churches, community outreach centers, provide food, water, and medical supplies to all in need. In His eyes it doesn't matter if they are your enemies or loved ones, we must do for all as we do for our own. We are a world community of the human race, one blood, one Lord, one baptism—a Global Family of born again believers.

*But if any provide not for his own, and specially for those of his own house,*

*he hath denied the faith, and is worse than an infidel.*
**1 Tim. 5:8** *(KJV)*

## WALK ACCORDING TO THE SPIRIT AND YOU WILL BE ABLE TO STAND UP

There is therefore now no condemnation to those who are in Christ Jesus, who do not walk according to the flesh, but according to the Spirit. For the law of the Spirit of life in Christ Jesus has made me free from the law of sin and death. For what the law could not do in that it was weak through the flesh, God did by sending His own Son in the likeness of sinful flesh, on account of sin: He condemned sin in the flesh, that the righteous requirement of the law might be fulfilled in us who do not walk according to the flesh but according to the Spirit. For those who live according to the flesh set their minds on the things of the flesh, but those who live according to the Spirit, the things of the Spirit. For to be carnally minded is death, but to be spiritually minded is life and peace. Because the carnal mind is enmity against God for it is not subject to the law of God, nor indeed can be. So then, those who are in the flesh cannot please God. But you are not in the flesh but in the Spirit, if indeed the Spirit of God dwells in you. Now if anyone does not have the Spirit of Christ, he is not His. And if Christ is in you, the body is dead because of sin, but the Spirit is life because of righteousness. But if the Spirit of Him who raised Jesus from the dead dwells in you, He who raised Christ from the dead will also give life to your mortal bodies through His Spirit who dwells in you. Therefore, brethren, we are debtors--not to the flesh, to live according to the flesh. For if you live according to the flesh you will die but if by the Spirit you put to death the deeds of the body, you will live.

**—Romans 8:1-13**

SIGNS OF THE END OF THE AGE

One of the reasons why in these last days we must stand up for Christ, is in view of the fact that the end is very, very near. Early one morning, in 2003, the Holy Spirit Himself woke me up at 7:17AM and spoke to me revealing specifically and clearly that Revelation chapter 18 is the prophecy toward America, *Political Babylon* when the church is gone. As you can recall there are two Babylon's of the Bible, political and religious. We are political Babylon. Sadaam Hussein, when he was alive, believed he was Nebuchadnezzar reincarnate. The palace that he lived in was about 1.9 billion dollars, and on the outside of the wall all the way around, which surrounded his palace, was engraved on every 30th brick, Nebuchadnezzar's face profile on the left side and on the opposite side, Sadaam Hussein's face profile. Undoubtedly, he was religious Babylon in his reign of power and authority, which exemplifies the verity that we are the political Babylon of Revelation 18.

Once more, in verse 4 of Revelation 18, you would find the words, "Come up out of her my people…" signifying the Rapture (Latin is *Rapiomore*; Greek is *Harpazo*). Therefore, we will not take part of the Tribulation or the Great Tribulation. So what is the difference between the two? The 1st Tribulation is the "Wrath of the Lamb" and the 2nd is the Great Tribulation, the "Wrath of God." The Lord will not allow His Bride to go through so much devastation and pandemonium, just like any husband who loves his wife will not allow such horror to come upon her. Here are several references proving the "Bride of Christ" will not go through this horrific episode:

*The voice of my beloved! Behold, He comes Leaping upon the mountains, Skipping upon the hills. My beloved is like a gazelle or a young stag. Behold, he stands behind our wall;* **He is looking through the windows** (Heaven), *Gazing through the lattice. My beloved spoke, and said to me:* **"Rise up, my love, my fair one, and come away** (Come up here!). *For lo, the winter is past, the rain is over and gone. The flowers appear on the earth; the time of singing has come, and the voice of the turtledove is heard in our land. The fig tree* (Israel) *puts forth her green figs, and the vines* with *the tender grapes give a good smell.* **Rise up, my love, my fair one, and come away** (Rapture: Come up here)!
**Song of Solomon 2:8-13** *(NKJV)* Emphasis added.

*But take heed to yourselves; lest your hearts be weighed down with carousing, drunkenness, and cares of this life, and that Day come on you unexpectedly. For it will come as a snare on all those who dwell on the face of the whole earth.* **Watch therefore, and pray always that you may**

**be counted worthy to escape all these things that will
come to pass, and to stand before the Son of Man**.
**Luke 21:34-36** *(NKJV)* Emphasis added.

*Behold, I tell you a mystery: We shall not all sleep, but we shall all be
changed--in a moment, in the twinkling of an eye, at the last trumpet. For*
**the trumpet will sound, and the dead will be raised
incorruptible, and we shall be changed**. *For this corruptible
must put on incorruption, and this mortal must put on immortality. So
when this corruptible has put on incorruption, and this mortal has put on
immortality, then shall be brought to pass the saying that is written: "Death is
swallowed up in victory." "O Death, where is your sting? O Hades, where is
your victory?"*
**1 Cor. 15:51-55** *(NKJV)* Emphasis added.

*For this we say to you by the word of the Lord, that we who are alive* and
*remain until the coming of the Lord will by no means precede those who are
asleep.* **For the Lord Himself will descend from heaven
with a shout**, *with the voice of an archangel, and with the trumpet of
God. And the dead in Christ will rise first.* **Then we who are alive
and remain shall be caught up together with them in
the clouds to meet the Lord in the air**. *And thus we shall
always be with the Lord. Therefore comfort one another with these words.*
**1 Thess. 4:15-18** *(NKJV)* Emphasis added.

*Looking for* **the blessed hope and glorious appearing of
our great God and Savior Jesus Christ**, *who gave Himself for
us, that He might redeem us from every lawless deed and purify for Himself
His own special people, zealous for good works.*
**Titus 2:13-14** *(NKJV)* Emphasis added.

**Because you have kept My command to persevere, I
also will keep you from the hour of trial, which shall
come upon the whole world**, *to test those who dwell on the earth.*
**Rev. 3:10** *(NKJV)* Emphasis added.

*And I heard another voice from heaven saying,* "**Come out of her, my people, lest you share in her sins, and lest you receive of her plagues**.
*Rev. 18:4 (NKJV)* Emphasis added.

As you mull over these Holy promises of God, remember Noah. The "King of the Universe" placed him in the ark and shut the door, saving him from the outside destruction where there was no life.

The Lord guided Lot and his two daughters out of Sodom and Gomorrah before He destroyed the cities with fire and brimstone, which his wife, Ado, died for looking back.

Before God decided to destroy Nineveh, He sent a prophet to warn them first, giving them an opportunity to come to repentance and be saved. Moreover, 150 years later as recorded in Nahum chapter 1 to 3, he explains the destruction of Nineveh for returning back to their sin. Although, they went back to their vomit (sin), if they would have stayed in a repented state, God will have kept His part of the deal.

Numerous occasions of God's **Agape'** love poured over the timeline of history, will prove His true attributes as a loving Father of all creation.

As I have pointed out earlier, we must get ready for Jesus' prominent return. There are 10,385 passages on eschatology alone; 27% of the Bible is the study of last things and the end of the age, as we know it. Out of that amount Beloved, their are one thousand prophecies in His Word, which five hundred of them has come to pass. The rest will be fulfilled as soon as we go home to be with the Lord. America and the rest of the world are so clueless and in such darkness, while the deception of Satan and his evil hordes are murdering, slaying, abusing, human trafficking, drugging, killing, all of our families, friends, people, and even Christians! As long as there is breath in my body, my wife and I will do ALL that we can in the mighty name of Jesus to lead hundreds of millions to our Lord and Savior Jesus the Christ! Watch and pray!

I pray that we will come together and love each other as we should, and lead people to The Savior of the world the best we know how. Rise up with me. No longer be labeled a Counterfeit Christian; let's not be artificial but faithful and true to God and one another. Follow me as I follow Christ and let's rise up together!

In Jesus name,

Rise up! His Pastors!

Rise up! His Evangelists!

Rise up! His Prophets!

Rise up! His Teachers!

Rise up! His Apostles!

Rise up! His Bishops, Deacons, Ministers, and the rest of the congregational members, lets take Dominion and the Kingdom by force!


BRINGING IT TOGETHER

The chapters you read were steps for new believers and the Well-seasoned. If you follow the pattern of the chapters, it all comes together so you would know to "guard your heart and spirit" empowering you to be able to go through "the valley of brokenness." Once you reach that level, the "fear of the Lord" can reign in your heart. When you fear the Lord, the Lord's Wisdom becomes part of your nature and then you can ask the Lord, "Who do you say that I am?" In the beginning of your salvation experience, you went to "the cross" and have become more than a "conqueror" in the eyes of the Lord, so you could worship the Only True Living God "in spirit and in truth," enabling you to fight the world's "lust" to "know your true purpose." Afterward, the "Living Water" has given you the cogency to be authentic; so when Jesus asks you, "Who here is on my side?" You can respond most assuredly with boldness and confidence as God allows "the real Christian to stand up" for Him!

## BE ENCOURAGED ALL IS GOING TO BE WELL

A WORD FROM GLORY TO THE NATIONS OF THE EARTH...Hallelujah! To the Lamb of God, who took away the sins of the world! I have so much hope for you and your entire family it burns within my members. Reader, I declare to you right now that your children and loved ones and those your are believing for to be saved, will return and come back home, and come back to the Spirit, giving their lives to Christ, and you will give God glory, because they will minister the Word of God to the lost in the end days, some will be saved and preach in the time of the tribulation, leading many to salvation! Nevertheless, they will receive their crown of Glory! Wait for it. It will come to pass!

### PROPHETIC WORD 2010

*The Lord Says, "My Spirit will reign in the earth, no one will forget who I AM. I AM the Almighty and Everlasting.*

*My voice will be known throughout every people, tongue, kindred, and nation. All things will submit to Me, from all places, all areas, all realms! America will come to turmoil and you will see her no more, after My Spirit brings revival for My children. I AM the Alpha & Omega, from Everlasting to Everlasting! No one will be able to hide from My presence, no one will escape from My blessings. The same will fall on those who are disobedient to Me, they will not be able to escape My presence, they will not be able to escape My judgment. Get prepared for my Coming, I AM building up My people who are called by My name and all those who answered the Call. My anointing and those who are anointed, will begin the revival for My Coming." Says the Lord of Hosts.*

**—Apostle Luis Lopez**

**Amen.**

# CONCLUSION

THE COUNTERFEIT CHRISTIAN has been a blessing, an honor, and a privilege to write. I thank God with all of my being for anointing me, and for opening this door, in taking part to help prepare the Body of Christ for the Second return of Jesus Christ.

I would like to say; it has been very challenging and an awesome experience having the ability to write to you, the Reader. You mean so much to me. I worked meticulously writing for many hours a day to make sure that what is written would be a huge blessing to you, as you read this right beside your Bible. The enemy has tried so hard to make sure this book did not make it into the hands of my publisher. Guess what? He lost again! Praise God!

Only by the grace of God and His anointing I am able to inscribe what He has put in my heart on paper. My prayer and hope is that you were left with just a little more knowledge, wisdom, and set thoughts to walk in peace and humility.

As you well know, I have gone through so much in my life. And there are many that would make what I went through very simplistic, but the focus of my conclusion is the fact of making sure, your walk with Christ would not be hindered nor your prayer life. Prayer is the weapon and life support of the believer.

In conclusion, allow yourself to seal these pages with new thoughts, a right spirit, and holy concepts; taking what God has already engineered into the pages of your own life. Never to travel in the path of becoming a counterfeit Christian, but to be a man, woman, or a young person, chasing after God. Always be aware of the enemy, so your focus can be consistently clear in knowing your true purpose of why you are here on earth. Filled with the love, power, compassion, mercy, and grace from the Holy Spirit, channeling through you upon others to be a blessing. He will always love you, and so do I, until the end of the age. May the Lord God truly bless you at all times and forevermore.

# ACKNOWLEDGMENTS

I would like to acknowledge a few new friends of mine, and those who have been there since the beginning.

**Julio E. Montalvo** (Kre8tor) I would like to thank you because you were the first one who led me to Christ back in 1987 when you spoke to me about the Book of Revelation while sitting on your dining room floor. It really scared me at first, after hearing you for a little while before the eyes of my heart opened and received understanding, and afterwards NO FEAR, thank God! I will never forget that day when we walked into your mother's living room when I stood in a circle hand-in-hand with your family, giving my life to Christ for the first time feeling the Holy Spirit literally move in my spirit. That was an awesome experience! Thank you sir, for leading me to the Lord. I will always be grateful to you, Betsy, Michelle, Eddie Sr., and Eddie Jr. that was an amazing day for me. I will always love you no matter what, I consider you like my real brother, always.

**Apostle John C. Ringold, Sr.**, and **Aquilla**, your wife. I would like to thank you both for the kindness, hospitality, and sincerity that you have demonstrated to my wife and I. We appreciate you, and love you both very much.

**Evangelist Donna**, my wife and I would like to thank you so much for being obedient to the voice of God and confirming what the Lord has spoken to us a few months earlier. I dedicate this book to you as well. You are loved and appreciated.

**Pastor Dan Willis**, at TCT, host of "I'M JUST SAYIN" television broadcast, and also to the entire TCT network, and the TCT television crew in Detroit, Michigan. Thank you all for your hospitality and the opportunity for us to be on your television program.

# ABOUT THE AUTHOR

Apostle Luis Lopez was born in Brooklyn, New York. He was brought up in the house of God. While he was still young, his grandmother taught him about Jesus Christ and how He would save people and change their lives significantly.

In the late 1980's Luis moved from Brooklyn, New York to Rochester, New York where he became a born again Christian at the age of 15. After serving the Lord for a while, he backslid for a season and experienced different influences in his life. The Holy Spirit kept him from the things of the world and never released him from His sight. He came back to the Lord afresh and still serving the Lord faithfully, 'til this day.

Apostles, prophets, pastors, and saints of the Lord, speak very vastly of him and his ministry. The moving of the Holy Spirit is evident in his life when he speaks. In fact, when Luis speaks it is apparent he has a teaching anointing, as the Spirit of the Lord leads him. He loves the Lord with all of his heart, soul, mind, and strength and yearns to win souls for the kingdom of God.

Luis Lopez has been married for more than 8 years to Michelle Lopez. They have four children.

He is an honest and dedicated man of God. His calling is specifically in the area of revelatory teaching, dreams, visions, and operates out of the five-fold ministry. He has been mandated and sent by the Lord Jesus to prepare the Body of Christ for the Second Advent of Christ, in parallel how God used John the Baptizer to prepare His people of the First Coming, so shall it be again. He was called and ordained as the Lord's apostle from his mother's womb.

In 2003, Jesus appeared to him in a vision and took him up in the spirit to the third heaven, seeing Christ seated on His Throne. Since this vision in 2003, he has been intensely receiving dreams, visions, and revelations. He has also received prophetic and audible dreams, visions, and divine revelation of the Word, the tribulation period and the end of the age.

# PRAYER OF SALVATION

Father, I am a sinner and I ask you to forgive me of my sins. Cleanse me with your blood and wash me from all unrighteousness. I believe that Jesus died on the cross for my sins and on the third day, You raised Him from the dead. Father, I ask you to fill me with your Holy Spirit right now, and write my name in the Lambs Book of Life. I give my entire life to you from this day onward. In Jesus name I pray. Amen.

**—ROMANS 10:9,10**

For speaking engagements and/or book signing contact:

www.apostleluislopez @yahoo.com

OR

www.prophetessmlopez @yahoo.com

Manufactured By:    RR Donnelley
Momence, IL  USA
June, 2010